Do Your Own Divorce in Maine

By: Pine Tree Legal Assistance, Inc.

Published and Printed by Freeport Village Press, Freeport, Maine 04032

1991 - Fourth Edition

There are many people who have helped us prepare this manual and put it into practice. Some must be named with special thanks:

Those who have helped most recently are:

Abused Women's Advocacy Project
Crystal Bond
Caring Unlimited
Rob Deschamps
Family Crisis Shelter
Family Support Center
Family Violence Project
Karmit Hyman, Esq.
Phyllis Hanson
Mary Henderson, Esq.
Georgia Houle
Lisa Markushewski
New Hope for Women
Jonathan Rogers, Esq.
Robert Mittel Esq.
Tammy Redlevske
Jody Soule
Spruce Run Association
Christopher St. John, Esq.
Womancare/Aegis
Womankind

Those who have also helped in the past are:

Thomas B. Benjamin, Esq.
Mary Browder
Susan Calkins, Esq.
Nancy Gentile
Rocki Graham
Nancy Fraser
Harriet Hunt, Esq.
Barbara Laughlin
Christopher Leighton, Esq.
Sandy Lizotte
Catherine G. Lucas
Sandra B. Lucas
Deborah Shaw Rice, Esq.
Karen Saum
Aryls J. Stritzel
Lucinda White, Esq.
Neville Woodruff, Esq.

and Charles E. Sherman, Esq., author of **HOW TO DO YOUR OWN DIVORCE IN CALIFORNIA**, from which we borrowed substantial ideas and text

and all people who have done or will in the future do their own divorces.

Prepared for Pine Tree Legal Assistance, Inc. by:
Christine B. Hastedt
Nan Heald, Esq.
Mary Henderson, Esq.

Illustrations by:
Jeanne Titherington

Cover illustration by:
Libby Barrett

Table of Contents

Table of Sample Completed Forms

Beginning

AN INTRODUCTION

This manual has been written for people who wish to get a divorce or are in the process of getting one. It was written with advice from a number of persons who have handled their own divorce without the help of a lawyer and others who are very familiar with divorce procedure in Maine.

In many cases getting a divorce in Maine is a very simple process which people find they can handle themselves. There are other cases, however, that are too complicated to be handled without the help of a lawyer. This manual will explain how to handle your own divorce, but it will also help you decide whether you can safely represent yourself or if you will need a lawyer's help.

Don't be discouraged by the size of this book. It is intended to provide information to people in many different situations. You will only need to read the parts of this book that apply to the facts of your case.

An immediate problem facing many people considering a divorce is expense. A large number of people needing a divorce simply can't afford one. Very poor people may qualify for free legal aid, but most legal aid offices suffer from too much business and not enough funding and are often unable to handle more than a fraction of the divorce cases that they are asked to take. Also, often there are people who are not poor enough to qualify for free legal aid, yet still can't afford an attorney. Today, many families live in such tight financial conditions that legal fees of several hundred dollars would be a severe hardship.

There are also many people in Maine who would like to feel that the process of getting divorced - like getting married - is one which they might control themselves. Our laws are made to seem so complicated that one is led to believe that he or she may not proceed safely without the help of various professionals. Hopefully, this manual will begin to dispel some of the mystique and confusion surrounding the law and give people the confidence to handle their own case, if that is their choice.

Some of what you will need to know is written in language that you may not now be familiar with. It is important to learn to understand and use these new terms since they will be used by the court clerk, the judge and others you will be talking to. This shouldn't discourage you. Most of what you read will be very understandable and this manual will help you become familiar with the rest.

If you begin to handle your divorce yourself and start to have problems or questions you can't resolve on your own, don't be afraid to call a lawyer. You can hire a lawyer just for the purpose of getting brief advice on a particular problem and then continue on with your divorce yourself. You can also decide at any point in the process that you need help and hire a lawyer to take over for you.

This manual will set out everything you will need to know in most cases to do your own divorce. But, before we get down to details, we'd like to give you a general idea of how the process works.

THE PROCEDURE

Either party to a marriage may decide that the marriage is simply intolerable or destructive to one of the partners in it. It is usually this person who decides that the only sensible way out is to go ahead with a divorce. This is a difficult decision which most people undertake only after a great deal of thought, and discussion with people who are close to them, and who can give them good advice and moral support.

A divorce begins with the preparing of a "Complaint". A Complaint is a legal paper that tells the court the basic facts of the marriage, the reason the person wants a divorce, and what he or she wants from the marriage once it is legally dissolved (e.g., custody, support, property division).

Along with the Complaint, a "Summons" is also prepared. This is simply a formal paper giving your spouse legal notice of the fact you are seeking a divorce and advising your spouse of his or her rights.

The court insists that your spouse be informed that you have filed for divorce and that he or she see a copy of the Complaint. The method for insuring that your spouse does know of the action is to have a copy of the Complaint and Summons "served" on him or her usually by a sheriff or by certified mail, depending on where he or she lives.

These technical terms - Summons, Complaint, service - will be discussed later on in this manual.

After the papers have been served, the "Plaintiff" (that spouse bringing the action) will "file" them at the District Court. Now the divorce has actually begun. It is at this point that the "Defendant" (the spouse against whom the action has been filed) may inform the court of his or her intention to contest the divorce. This will be done by an "Answer". Most people who will be using this manual will bring divorce actions which will not be contested and therefore there will usually be no Answer.

There is a sixty-day waiting period after service before the divorce can be "heard" in court. The "hearing" is a very simple proceeding and usually lasts no more than ten to fifteen minutes. Although most people feel nervous about the hearing itself, with careful preparation there is no need to. Chapter 15 of this manual explains fully how to prepare for court, and also recommends that you go to the court before your divorce hearing and watch and listen to other divorces being heard.

Generally, the judge will indicate at the time of the hearing whether or not he or she will grant the divorce. Unless some great mistake has been made (and this manual should keep you from making any great mistake), your divorce will be granted on that day. However, there is an appeal period following the hearing and the divorce does not become final for ten days, unless both you and your spouse sign a special court form which says you do not intend to appeal.

In the final Order granting your divorce, the judge will divide family property that is considered "marital property". Decisions about property cannot be changed later on (except under exceptional circumstances and these are hard to prove). The judge will also make orders regarding custody, visitation and child support, but these things are not necessarily finally resolved by the divorce. If circumstances change substantially after the divorce becomes final, then either spouse can ask the Court to amend the Divorce Order to change the original ruling in some way.

SOME WORDS OF WARNING

Not everyone who picks up this manual should go ahead and do his or her own divorce. There are some people whose marital situation is just too complicated to be dissolved without professional assistance. While it is true that a judge will rarely refuse to grant a divorce itself to two people who have a valid reason for wanting one, in most cases several other issues must be resolved in the context of a divorce action as well. It is with these other issues - such as property, custody, alimony - that problems may arise. Generally, where substantial amounts of property are involved, or where there is a conflict over who will have custody of the child(ren), a lawyer's help will be needed. These considerations are discussed more fully in Chapters 2 and 6 of this manual.

We must also caution you about the changing nature of the law itself. In every legislative session there are a number of changes that are made in the State's body of laws. It is possible that the Legislature may make changes in Maine's divorce law that will affect what is written in this manual. Also, from time to time court forms may change. Court clerks may be helpful to you in both these situations. The clerks will not be able to give you legal advice because they are not attorneys and it would be unlawful for them to do so. But they can help you with matters relating to process and filing of papers. Don't be afraid to ask questions. In our experience, clerks are usually pleasant and helpful.

This manual is divided into three sections. Part One will explain the terms and legal principles that you will need to know before actually beginning. It is important to read these pages carefully so you will not make any mistakes when filling out the papers.

Detailed instructions for filling out the papers will be found in Part Two of the manual. You might want to look at these forms first, but do not attempt to fill them out until you have studied Part One carefully.

Part Three provides information to those people who have special problems in connection with their divorce. Chapter 18 deals with the need for court action **before** the divorce is final and Chapter 19 deals with the need for court action to change the judgment **after** the divorce is final.

PART ONE

Some Things to Learn Before You Start

Chapter 1

Your Right to Represent Yourself

Pro se is a Latin phrase for representing yourself in court. It is pronounced "PRO-SAY".

Pro se divorces are no longer a new thing in Maine. The first one that we know of was done in 1972 and many hundreds have been done since then. In fact, several thousand copies of this manual have been sold since it was first published in 1975. It is now common to walk into a courtroom in Maine on divorce day and find a person doing his of her own divorce. Court personnel and judges have gotten used to the idea, and people doing their own divorces are finding the procedure quite easy provided they are well prepared. Pro se divorces are also being done successfully in many other parts of the country.

You have an absolute right to represent yourself in court on any legal matter, including divorce. Maine law states that you **must** be allowed to represent yourself:

> "Parties may plead or manage their own cases in court or do so by the aid of counsel as they see fit to employ." 4 M.R.S.A. § 860.

Further, you must be allowed to purchase court papers that you need from the clerk of court and the clerk must accept them when you return to file them.

Chapter 2

Should I Do My Own Divorce?

So, the answer to the question of whether you **may** represent yourself is "Yes". The next question that must be asked is "should I represent myself?"

From our experience we feel you should represent yourself only when you expect no opposition from your spouse. You may have been separated from your spouse for a long time or for some reason he or she has no particular interest in what you do about the marriage. In such cases you will probably have an easy time of doing your own divorce.

It is very common, particularly in cases where there has been a long separation, or a difficult marriage, to be uncertain of just how your spouse will react.

In such cases you could start the divorce and see what happens when your spouse is confronted with the reality of court action. If your spouse gets a lawyer, you can hire one too. In fact, if you run into problems anytime after starting your own divorce, you can hire a lawyer to help you.

In cases where your spouse is in the picture and you have discussed the issues in the divorce with each other, it is important that you be able to agree upon (or at least be fairly sure that your spouse won't contest) the following:

- that you should get divorced
- who is to have custody of the child(ren)

* how visitation is to be arranged, at least generally
* how much is to be paid for child support
* how much is to be paid for alimony
* how to divide the property and bills which you have accumulated during the marriage

If you have a lot of property, especially if it is in the form of stocks and bonds, real estate, or an interest in a business, you should seriously consider having professional advice (at least for purposes of working out a divorce settlement). In a situation where there are sizeable assets, tax considerations will arise and you may need the help of a lawyer with them.

This is especially important because property decisions are final and cannot be changed once the Court has granted your divorce (except in very limited circumstances and these are very difficult to prove). In this way, those decisions are different from ones about child custody and child support, which **can** be changed later on, if either spouse can show that circumstances have substantially changed since the date of the divorce.

You should be aware that bringing a divorce action becomes more complicated when you don't know where your spouse is, or if he or she is in the military service. The particular procedures that you must follow in these situations are described in Chapter 11 of this manual. If you have either a missing or military spouse you should read this chapter carefully before deciding whether or not you should represent yourself.

Although not illegal, it is not advisable for you to do your own divorce while you are pregnant. The judge may, and probably will, refuse to hear the case until you have had the child. This is because no custody or support order may be issued for a child who is not yet born. Since it is the right of that child to receive support from both parents, the judge will want to postpone the hearing until he or she is able to make a support order for that child. If a judge does hear the case in this situation, he or she will not order custody and support for the unborn child, Another court action will be necessary after the child has been born for these orders to be made.

If you are hesitant about doing your own divorce but feel that financially you have no choice, you may have another option. Maine law permits the court to order one spouse to pay the attorney's fees for the other in a divorce action in cases where one has the clear ability to pay and the other does not. If you want to pursue this possibility you will have to find a lawyer willing to represent you under this kind of arrangement.

Although most lawyers ask for at least some part of their fee from their client, this practice varies considerably. You may want to talk to several law offices about the kind of fee arrangement they are willing to make with you. In these discussions, explain your own financial situation and your spouse's and ask the attorney if he or she would be willing to take all or part of the fee from your spouse. After you've made a number of phone calls, you will be in a better position to make the choice between hiring a lawyer and representing yourself.

The final decision as to whether to represent yourself is your own. If you are uncertain, it may help to read the rest of this manual before making a decision. If you are nervous because you've never done anything like this before, remember that lots of people have done their own divorce in Maine before you. Many of them felt just as you do at the beginning. Consider going to the court on a day when divorces are being heard just to watch. It may help you to feel more comfortable with the process.

Chapter 3

Jurisdiction and Venue

You will encounter the words "jurisdiction" and "venue" when doing your own divorce. Although no one will ask you to give a legal definition of them, you should have a basic understanding of what they mean.

JURISDICTION

"Jurisdiction" in your divorce case means that a Maine Court has the power to grant you a divorce.

The court has jurisdiction if **any** of the following is true:

a. The plaintiff (the person starting the divorce action) has lived in Maine for six months before beginning the divorce; or

b. The plaintiff is a resident[1] of the State **and** the parties were married here; or

---

[1] "Resident" means that the person is in Maine now and plans to stay here. It does not require that a person has lived here for a particular length of time. A person becomes a resident on the day he or she arrives in Maine, provided he or she plans to stay here.

c. The plaintiff is a resident of the State **and** the parties lived in Maine when the reasons for the divorce developed; or

d. The defendant (the spouse against whom the divorce is being brought) is a resident of Maine.

VENUE

"Venue" determines which court within the State will hear your divorce. It is in this court that you will purchase your legal papers, file them and appear for your hearing.

To find out which court has venue of your divorce, match up the town where you **or** your spouse lives (your choice), with the court that serves that area. Use the Court and County Locator in the Appendix of this manual. You will go to the Civil Division of the District Court which will be serving you. (Note: If you are a member of the Penobscot or Passamaquoddy Indian tribes, read the discussion of tribal court below.)

If you are planning to move but are not sure where or when, it is all right to file papers in the court serving the area where you are presently living and then return there on the day of the hearing. You need only consider where either you or your spouse is residing at the **beginning** of proceedings; in other words, where you will be at the time that papers are "served" on your spouse.

TRIBAL COURT

If both you **and** your spouse are members of the Penobscot Indian Nation or the Passamaquoddy Tribe and you are considered residents by your tribe, then you should obtain your forms and file your divorce Complaint in tribal court.

If you have any questions about whether you should file in Maine District Court or in tribal court, check with your tribe's tribal court clerk.

The address of the tribal court for the Penobscot Indian Nation is:

Clerk of Court
Penobscot Tribal Court
6 River Road
Indian Island
Old Town, Maine 04468

The address of the tribal court for both the Passamaquoddy reservations is:

Clerk of Court
Passamaquoddy Tribal Court
Pleasant Point Reservation
P.O. Box 351
Perry, Maine 04667

Chapter 4

Grounds for Divorce

There are really three partners to a marriage - the two persons who have decided that they want to be married and the State of Maine. The State gives its consent to a marriage by allowing a license to be issued.

In a divorce action there are also three parties, the State once again being the third. The State, through its court system, wants to insure that all of its laws are followed before granting a divorce. The State will only consent to a divorce for certain specific reasons. Those reasons are called "grounds".

There are a number of reasons - "grounds" - that the State recognizes as good ones for granting a divorce. Of these, "Irreconcilable Marital Differences" is most commonly used. "Cruel and Abusive Treatment," although next in number, is far less commonly used today. The remaining grounds are only used in a very few cases each year. Although we have listed below all of the grounds for divorce available under Maine law, you will probably want to pay the closest attention to Irreconcilable Marital Differences. Cruel and Abusive Treatment is used much less these days. The other grounds are quite technical and require very specific proof, making handling your own divorce much more difficult.

In Maine a divorce may be granted for any one of the following reasons:

* Irreconcilable Marital Differences
* Cruel and Abusive Treatment
* Adultery
* Impotence
* Extreme Cruelty
* Utter Desertion continued for three consecutive years prior to filing of the Complaint for divorce
* Gross and Confirmed habits of intoxication from the use of intoxicating liquors, opium or other drugs
* Nonsupport, where one spouse being of sufficient ability to provide for the other, grossly, wantonly or cruelly refuses or neglects to provide suitable maintenance for the complaining spouse
* Mental Illness requiring confinement in a mental institution for at least seven consecutive years prior to the beginning of the action

While proof of any of these grounds can get you a divorce, we recommend using Irreconcilable Marital Differences if you plan to do your own divorce. We also have included a description of "cruel and abusive treatment." Some battered spouses and others may want to use this ground because they feel it best describes their reasons for wanting the divorce.

If, after reading the description of both these grounds below, you do not feel that your situation fits within either, and you think it might better fit within one of the other grounds listed above, then it is probably best to contact a lawyer. You'll notice however, as you read further, that there is some overlapping among the grounds. In most cases, you should be able to use "irreconcilable marital differences", even if your problem seems to be more specifically addressed by one of the others.

For example, while there are specific grounds dealing with refusal to provide support and excessive drinking, these problems may also be used as proof of Irreconcilable Marital Differences. In such a case, using the more common ground would make it easier to represent yourself.

Before choosing between Irreconcilable Marital Differences and Cruel and Abusive Treatment, you should consider several factors, both legal and practical.

If you use Cruel and Abusive Treatment, you are saying that your spouse was more at fault than you in causing the divorce, and that you have been injured by his or her actions.

If you choose Irreconcilable Marital Differences, you are saying that no one person is more at fault or has been more injured than the other.

This basic legal difference gives rise to a number of practical considerations.

First, you might find that your spouse is less likely to contest a divorce based on Irreconcilable Marital Differences because you would not be **blaming** him or her for the problems in the marriage.

Also the ground of Irreconcilable Marital Differences might be easier to prove because, although it is based on your very serious disagreement, you need not prove that your spouse actually mistreated you.

However, it may be important to you to use the ground of Cruel and Abusive Treatment proving that your spouse was at fault in destroying your marriage.

A more specific description of the two most commonly used grounds for divorce follows:

a. Irreconcilable Marital Differences

This is the ground most often used. If you use it, you must show the court that:

A. There are serious problems in your marriage;

B. These problems cannot be resolved; and

C. As a result of the problems the marriage has completely broken down.

In order to prove the above, your testimony in court should include the following specific information:

* the approximate date that you and your spouse separated for the final time;
* what the serious problems were in your marriage;
* what attempts were made to hold the marriage together (e.g., formal counseling, discussions with friends and family members, serious discussions between yourselves);
* why these attempts were unsuccessful; and
* that you believe that there is no hope of saving the marriage.

Probably the best advice that can be given to a person using this ground is to approach the matter very seriously. Present the court with problems that are real and substantial. The judge will want to know that the problems were recurring or part of a pattern, not just an isolated instance of disagreement. Problems such as continued differences over the use of money, about educational or work plans, over the philosophy of child rearing or even whether or not to have children at all, are ones which the court is likely to take seriously. But most importantly, it must appear that there is no hope whatsoever for resolving the differences, that you have tried, but the marriage cannot be saved.

It is important that the differences between you and your spouse were ones that developed during the marriage, and not ones that you were aware of beforehand. For example, if you and your spouse disagreed about whether to have children before you were married, but married anyhow, it would not be advisable to rely on this disagreement in testifying that your marriage has broken down as a result of Irreconcilable Marital Differences.

In Part II of this manual you will find both an example of how the Complaint form should be prepared using this ground and a sample of the kind of testimony that a person using this ground might give at a divorce hearing.

b. Cruel and Abusive Treatment

Although next in number, this ground is no longer commonly used. If you use Cruel and

Abusive Treatment, you **must** show the judge two things:

A. That your spouse has abused you and treated you cruelly;

B. That this has caused you physical and/or mental injury and if the marriage is continued, it would jeopardize your physical and/or mental health

In other words, cause and effect is required. **Cause,** your spouse's cruel treatment of you, brings about an **effect,** the physical and/or mental harm or distress caused you.

It is extremely important to show the judge **both** the **cause** and its **effect** on you in your testimony, or he or she will not be able to find sufficient evidence to grant your divorce.

The Cruel and Abusive Treatment of your spouse (the **cause**) may include such actions as:

* Refusal to talk with you
* Refusal to support you
* Belittling you or insulting you in front of friends or relatives
* Sexual involvement with other men or women
* Excessive drinking or drug abuse
* Going out all night without telling you where he or she is going
* Arguing a lot
* Slapping, shoving or grabbing you
* Hitting or beating you
* Sexual relations that you didn't want to engage in
* Your spouse's treatment of your children, i.e., lack of interest, ignoring your children, punishing them too frequently or too severely

The second part of your case will be the **effect** that your spouse's behavior had on you. This could include a variety of things, such as:

* Emotional strain - headaches from the tension of living with your spouse
* Bruises, broken bones, physical scars
* Hysteria (constant and uncontrollable sobbing)
* Excessive loss or gaining of weight
* Loss of sleep
* Bad temper
* Extreme nervousness - if your doctor ever prescribed nerve pills, this should be mentioned
* Excessive cigarette smoking - more than before this marriage started to fail
* Depression

* Avoidance of normal social contact
* Inability to function normally because of marital problems
* Study your life before and after your marriage began to go bad. The bad changes are all things that could be caused by problems with your marriage.

In Part II of this manual you will find an example of how the Complaint form should be prepared using this ground and a sample of the kind of testimony that a person using this ground might give. If you are planning to use "cruel and abusive treatment" as a ground for your divorce, you should probably also check off "irreconcilable marital differences" as a ground on the Complaint. This way, if the judge doesn't think that you have proved "cruel and abusive treatment", he or she should still find that there are grounds for the divorce in "irreconcilable marital differences."

Chapter 5

Collusion and Condonation

COLLUSION

In order to get your divorce, you must show that there has been no "collusion".

Collusion means making a secret agreement or cooperating for a fraudulent or deceitful purpose. What this means in terms of a divorce is that, if you do not have a ground (reason that the state recognizes as legitimate for getting a divorce), you and your spouse can't sit down, decide you want a divorce, and make up a story that does give you grounds.

It does not mean that you can't sit down together and resolve the things that need to be resolved in order to split up. It is also all right to agree with your spouse to use the ground of Irreconcilable Marital Differences, as long as those differences really exist.

The judge cannot grant your divorce if he or she finds collusion. This means that you and your spouse can't agree to tell the judge about incidents and problems that didn't exist in order to get out of the marriage.

CONDONATION

The judge will want to be certain that you have made a serious, thoughtful and firm decision to end the marriage and that you are not likely to change your mind. One thing he or she may consider is whether there has been any "condonation". Although you should know what this word means, it is unlikely to be mentioned at the divorce hearing.

Condonation means that you, being aware of your spouse's bad treatment of you, willingly and completely forgave him or her. Condonation acts like an eraser, wiping out your spouse's previous bad actions.

A common example of condonation is when you file for divorce and then get back together with your spouse for a period of time. "Getting together" basically means living together again and/or having sexual relations with the intention of unconditionally renewing your relationship.

However, if you got back together again for a trial period, under certain agreed-upon conditions, and those conditions were violated, it is unlikely that a judge would find that there had been condonation. For example, if you took your spouse back because he said he wouldn't hit you again, and then he did, a judge would be very unlikely to find that condonation had occurred.

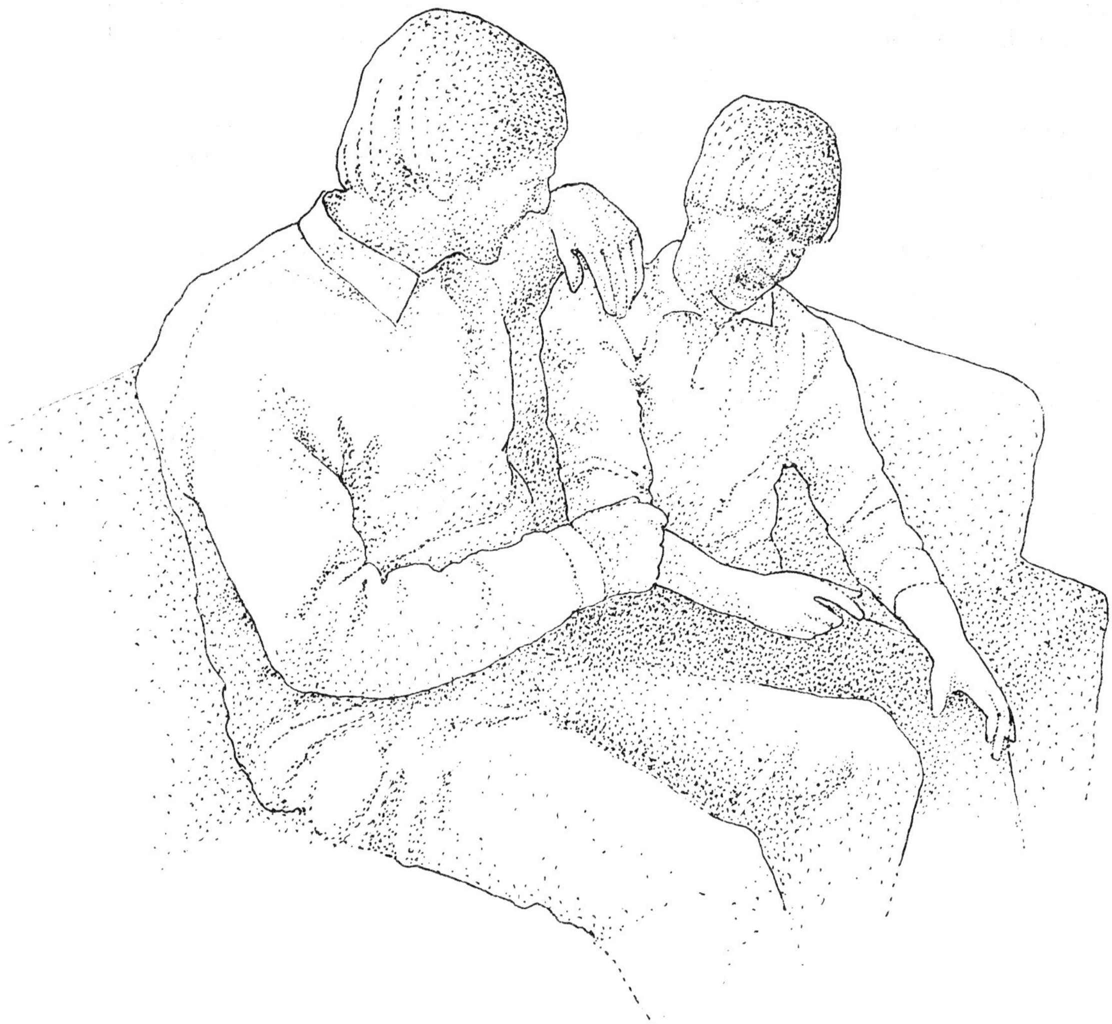

Chapter 6

Relief

(or Custody, Visitation, Child Support, Alimony, Division of Property, Bills, Restoration of Maiden Name, Attorney Fees, Health Insurance)

a. INTRODUCTION

If you have good grounds for divorce and there has been no collusion or condonation, the judge will grant you your divorce. However, the judge will want to do more than that. He or she will want to decide about every part of the marriage relationship, which is ending with the divorce. Who is going to be responsible for seeing to it that the children are adequately clothed and fed? How is visitation going to be worked out? Who is going to be legally responsible for the children? Who is going to keep what property? If one spouse is going to have little or no income, how will that spouse survive after the divorce?

This chapter explains how you should go about resolving these questions. What you decide to ask the court for is called "relief".

You will ask the court for the particular relief that you want at the end of the Complaint in a section called the "Prayer".

The prayer looks like this:

WHEREFORE, Plaintiff prays that a divorce from the bonds of matrimony between Plaintiff and Defendant be adjudged;

That the parental rights and responsibilities regarding the minor child(ren), including child support payments, be determined;

That the Court set apart to each party his or her property and divide the marital property pursuant to Title 19, M.R.S.A. § 722-A;

That reasonable alimony, or a specific sum in lieu thereof, be ordered paid to Plaintiff by Defendant;

That reasonable counsel fees be ordered paid by Defendant to ______________________________
Attorney for Plaintiff, execution to issue therefor when decree of divorce is granted; and

That Plaintiff be allowed to change her name to ______________________________.

Depending on what you are asking for, you will either simply leave the printed line as it is or change it to reflect what you want.

We will discuss each section of the prayer separately in this chapter.

You should also consider whether you need to have the judge decide some of these issues immediately, on a temporary basis, until the divorce hearing takes place. If you need immediate help with these issues after the Complaint is filed, you will need to file a "Motion Pending Divorce." This is discussed in Chapter 18.

Finally, you should realize that the final divorce order will affect the requested "relief" in different ways. Your marriage will be ended by the divorce; you will be a single person again and free to re-marry. The division of property (including marital property and bills owed by both spouses) will be final in the divorce order (except in very limited circumstances and these are hard to prove. See Chapter 20 for these exceptions). BUT, certain other things can be changed later on, by going back to court and requesting that the court "modify" the Divorce Judgment. These kinds of things include everything affecting the children of your marriage (including custody, child support and visitation). If some amount of alimony was ordered in your divorce judgment, you can also ask that it be changed later on. (But if no alimony was ordered in the divorce judgment, you cannot later ask for some). In order for the court to modify the divorce judgment, you must show that "circumstances have substantially changed" since the divorce order became final. This process is discussed in more detail in Chapter 19, "Post Divorce Motions."

b. PARENTAL RIGHTS & RESPONSIBILITIES/CUSTODY

Introduction

In 1983, the Maine Legislature passed a new law affecting the relationship between divorcing parents and their children. This law has changed both the words used to describe the idea of custody and the way parents and the court make decisions about children in a divorce case.

Divorce Orders no longer refer to "custody"; instead, the order will describe "parental rights and responsibilities" with respect to the children under 18. Responsibility may be assigned to either or both parents for the following:

- primary physical residence of the child(ren)
- parent-child contact (visitation)
- support
- education
- medical and dental care
- religious upbringing
- travel boundaries and expenses

These rights and responsibilities can be all assigned to one parent, who would make all major decisions for the child(ren). This is called "sole parental rights and responsibilities." If both parents share the decisions and consult before making any major decision about the child(ren), this is called "shared parental rights and responsibilities." You can also "allocate" (assign) certain kinds of decisions to one parent, and other kinds of decisions to the other.

Deciding how to resolve parental rights and responsibilities for the children is often one of the most difficult parts of splitting up. It is a decision which concerns the future welfare of both you and your children. This section will help you consider the many factors involved in making this decision.

The fact that you have children does not mean that you can't or shouldn't do your own divorce. What it does mean is that you must put some more thought into that question.

If you and your spouse can agree on parental rights and responsibilities (or at least you know he or she won't contest it in court), then you should have no difficulty doing your own divorce. However, if your spouse will actively contest your request for custody, you may need a lawyer's help. You will also be required to go to mediation with a court-appointed mediator. This process is discussed in Chapter 13.

Jurisdiction

A judge can make an enforceable custody order only if the Maine court has "jurisdiction" over the child; in other words, the legal authority to make such a decision.

If you have already established jurisdiction for the divorce itself, (see Chapter 3), it is likely that the court will also have the authority to decide who will get custody of your children.

However, if another state has already made a custody order involving the child, or if the child has been living outside of Maine for an extended period of time, it would be wise to speak with a lawyer about this issue before proceeding.

In order to prove to the court that it does have jurisdiction over the children and can make a custody order affecting them, you must prepare an affidavit as required by the Uniform Child Custody Jurisdiction Act and file it with the court. This form must be prepared in all cases in which the court is being asked to make a custody order. (Remember, custody orders in a divorce only cover children from your current marriage.)

This form is available for purchase from the court. Instructions on how to fill out this form appear in Chapter 10 and a copy of the blank form appears in the Appendix.

This affidavit should be served on your spouse along with the Divorce Complaint and Summons. Further instructions about service and filing appear at Chapters 11 and 12.

If you are required to serve your spouse with a copy of the affidavit, ordinarily he or she will learn your current address. (Of course, if you have a post office box and use this as your address, this is not a problem for you.) If this creates a danger to your own safety or that of your children, talk to the court clerk **before** filling in the forms.

Sole Parental Rights and Responsibilities

If you are granted sole parental rights and responsibilities, you will be the parent with legal responsibility for the children. You will have the major responsibility for their raising, housing and care, and you will have the last word in any decisions involving them.

Shared Parental Rights and Responsibilities

Shared parental rights and responsibilities means that the legal responsibility for the children is shared. This is also called "joint custody" although Maine courts don't use this term anymore. This means that both you and your spouse will share equally in any decisions involving the children. You will each have an equal right to decide where the children will live and you will be entitled to share equally in decisions concerning schooling, religion, extra-curricular activities, and all other things affecting their welfare. You will each have the right to read and review your children's school and medical records.

You can request shared parental rights and responsibilities even though you want the children to live with one parent. If this is the case, you should ask the court to make either your home or your spouse's home the children's "primary residence".

Some people want to have the children spend an equal amount of time with each parent. In this case, there will be no "primary residence" for the children. You can ask the court to spell out the specific arrangement you want in the final order.

In recent years more couples have asked the court to award shared parental rights and responsibilities. Many believe it to be a more positive approach to child rearing and a way to minimize the personal difficulties that arise between the parties when a custody decision must be made. After all, many divorces these days are a result of people simply not getting along with each other, rather than one partner being a villain. In such cases, each parent believes that they are both equally suited to raise the children, and shared parental rights and responsibilities seems to be the solution.

Realistically speaking, however, shared parental rights and responsibilities may prove to be a difficult arrangement to live with. If you are considering it, read the following paragraphs carefully.

The basic objection to shared parental rights and responsibilities is that it requires two people, unable to get along in marriage, to continue to share decision-making about what is best for the children. Before making up your mind, consider the following questions.

1. Do you think your spouse is a good parent? Does your spouse think you are a good parent?

2. Who has been primarily responsible for taking care of the children during the marriage? Is it realistic to consider sharing this responsibility after the divorce?

3. Is there a lot of anger, hostility or resentment right now between you and your spouse because of the divorce? Will you each be able to put those feelings aside when you have to talk about the children?

4. Will you be able to talk to each other and make decisions about the children, on an emergency and regular basis in the future?

5. What arrangement will be best for the children?

Allocated Parental Rights and Responsibilities

If you aren't comfortable in sharing all major decisions about your children in the future with your spouse - as you would be required to do if "shared parental rights and responsibilities" were ordered by the judge - you may want to consider asking for "allocated parental rights and responsibilities".

"Allocated parental rights and responsibilities" means that the parent with whom the children are living will make all decisions affecting the children except for those kinds of decisions which have been specifically "allocated" by the judge for **both** parents to share. For example, you may want to share responsibility with your spouse in making decisions about the children's religious upbringing or education, but not about anything else. If the judge then orders that parental rights and responsibilities for the children's religious upbringing and education be shared, you will be required to reach agreement with your spouse before taking any action on these issues. If the judge does not specifically allocate responsibility in a given area, then those decisions are up to you.

Finally, as with shared parental rights and responsibilities, be sure that you and your spouse can work together in making decisions before you agree to share any types of decision making for the children.

How the Court Will Decide Custody

In any type of arrangement, the court must make an order that is based on the best interest of the children. In making this decision, the court is required to consider the following:

A. The age of the child;

B. The relationship of the child with the child's parents and any other persons who may significantly affect the child's welfare;

C. The preference of the child, if old enough to express it;

D. The duration and adequacy of the child's current living arrangements and the desirability of maintaining continuity;

E. The stability of any proposed living arrangements for the child;

F. The motivation of the parties involved and their capacities to give the child love, affection and guidance;

G. The child's attachment to the child's present home, school and community;

H. The capacity of each parent to allow and encourage frequent and continuing contact between the child and the other parent, including physical access;

I. The capacity of each parent to cooperate or to learn to cooperate in child care;

J. Methods for assisting parental cooperation and resolving disputes and each parent's willingness to use those methods;

K. The effect on the child if one parent has sole authority over the child's upbringing; and

L. All other factors having a reasonable bearing on the physical and psychological well-being of the child.

If you are considering shared parental rights and responsibilities, the best evidence to present to the court is a proven track record. The judge is much more likely to award shared parental rights and responsibilities if you have had this type of arrangement during your separation and it has worked well.

Nuts and Bolts — Custody

As mentioned previously, child custody decisions may be difficult. You might try different living arrangements for your children even before filing for divorce to help you make up your mind about whether to seek shared, sole, or allocated parental rights and responsibilities and about which visitation arrangements work best. You might agree to short trial periods in which one or more of the children would try living with the other spouse. It may be helpful to involve the children, other relatives or mutual friends in resolving this question. Sometimes professional counseling or consultation with a member of the clergy may be helpful.

You do not have to specify the kind of custody arrangement that you want in the Complaint. In the prayer (at the end of the Complaint) you will see the following printed request:

> "That the parental rights and responsibilities regarding the minor child(ren), including child support payments, be determined;"

If you have children from this marriage, simply leave this request as it is. If you have no children, you will cross it out.

On the day of the hearing, you will be required to tell the judge what kind of custody arrangement that you want ordered. The judge will probably ask if you and your spouse have reached an agreement on this issue. If you have, simply tell the judge that you agree. If your spouse has not been in contact with you since the divorce was filed and shows no interest in the children, tell that to the judge.

If you and your spouse cannot agree about custody, the law requires that you go to mediation before the divorce hearing, except in exceptional cases. Mediation is discussed in Chapter 13 of this manual.

c. PARENT-CHILD CONTACT/VISITATION

The parent who is not going to be living with the child or children is almost always given the right of reasonable visitation (unless it is reasonably felt that he or she presents some sort of danger to the children or may take off with them). Thus, subject to the approval of the parent having custody, the other parent is entitled to visit at reasonable times and places with reasonable notice.

If visitation is ordered by the court, you are not entitled to forbid it for any reason other than the well-being of the children. If your spouse shows up to visit in a drugged, drunken or highly emotional condition it would be reasonable to prevent the visit **on that occasion**. However, if he or she has at some time angered you, or even if he has not supported the children, you are **not** entitled to prevent visits for these reasons.

Restricted Visitation

There may be a reason that you want visitation to be supervised or restricted in the court order itself. If so, you must specifically request this limitation at the hearing. If you have good reason, the judge may order that your spouse only be allowed to visit during certain hours on certain days, or only in the presence of a third party. Perhaps your spouse has an alcohol or drug problem or has mistreated the children or you in the past. In such cases restricted or supervised visitation may be justified.

It is extremely difficult to get the judge to order no visitation. You must show strong proof that no good would come from such visits. For example, in cases where your spouse has sexually abused the children or caused serious physical harm to them, an order prohibiting visitation would be warranted.

Nuts and Bolts — Visitation

You do not have to specify the kind of visitation that you want in the Complaint. (However, if you want to specify this in the Complaint, you can.) When you ask the court in your prayer to determine the "parental rights and responsibilities regarding the minor child(ren)", you are also asking the court to determine what visitation will be ordered. If you think you and your spouse will have difficulty working out a visitation schedule on your own, you may want to ask the judge at your hearing to set specific dates, times, and/or places where the visits will take place. This may avoid arguments in the future. Otherwise, the judge will probably order "reasonable visitation". This assumes regular and frequent contact and means that you will have to work out specific dates, times and places on your own. You may also want to request restricted visitation as discussed above. If you do, you must make this request at your hearing as well.

Remember that the visitation arrangement ordered in your divorce judgment can be changed later on if you can show the court that "circumstances have changed substantially" since the original order was made. The process of changing a divorce judgment is described in Chapter 19.

d. CHILD SUPPORT

Introduction

The obligation of a parent to support his or her child is commonly accepted and is required by law. It has high priority both in the law and in the minds of the judges. This duty usually lasts until the child turns 18.

If a child dies, marries or joins the military before he or she turns 18, then the obligation to support the child ends when that event occurs. If a child is still in school when he or she turns 18, the parent with whom the child is living can ask the court for the support obligation to continue until the child graduates, withdraws or is expelled from school, or turns 19 (whichever happens first).

If there are children involved in the divorce, the judge will want to make an order for support. Even if your spouse is unable to pay support at the time of the divorce because he or she is unemployed, you should nevertheless request support, so you will have an order to rely on when his or her circumstances change.

Jurisdiction

In order for an enforceable support order to be made against your spouse, the court must have legal authority over him or her. This is called having jurisdiction, or more precisely, **jurisdiction in personam**.

If your spouse is in the State of Maine at the time the action is begun, the court will have jurisdiction and any support order will therefore be enforceable.

If your spouse is not in Maine, you can get an enforceable support order if:

1. personal service, instead of certified mail service, is made (see Chapter 11 for further information on service), **and**
2. **(a)** you and your spouse maintained a home together in Maine, **or**

   (b) the problems causing the divorce developed while your spouse was living in Maine.

Gaining jurisdiction over an out-of-state spouse can be a somewhat confusing area in the law. If you have a problem with it you may want to consider seeing a lawyer.

If You Receive Public Assistance

Do you or your spouse receive, have you received, or are you likely to receive Aid to Families with Dependent Children (AFDC), or Medicaid? If so, then the Maine Department of Human Services has an interest in your support order. This is because when you or your spouse receive this assistance you give or "assign" to the State of Maine the right to receive your child support. The Maine Department of Human Services then collects the support and distributes it in a way that allows the State to keep some of the support for reimbursement for some or all of the AFDC or Medicaid it has paid.

As you can see from the form Complaint for Divorce (Form 1), you must state in the Complaint whether you or your spouse have received or are likely to receive public assistance (AFDC or Medicaid) for your children. If you or your spouse have received, are receiving, or are likely to receive public assistance for your children, then you must notify the Maine Department of Human Services when you file your Complaint in the court by sending a copy of your Complaint for Divorce to:

Central Office Supervisor
Division of Support Enforcement
Department of Human Services
State House Station #11
Augusta, Maine 04333

Many courts require you to also file a "Certificate of Notice" form indicating that you have sent a copy of your divorce Complaint to the Department of Human Services. Ask your court clerk if this form is required. If necessary, Form 6 can be used for this purpose. The Department of Human Services may become involved in your divorce, but this should not affect your ability to represent yourself.

You must also notify the Department of the actual hearing date and time. Someone from DHS may come to the hearing, to offer their opinion on what "reasonable child support" should be in your case.

Nuts and Bolts — Support

The amount of child support will be determined by the judge, based on guidelines which apply to every divorce in Maine. Just as with custody, you do not have to specify the amount of support in the Complaint. The printed form asks that "child support payments be determined." If you have children from this marriage, you will leave these words as they are.

The court clerk will provide you with an "Affidavit of Income and Assets" and a "Child Support Worksheet". Child support is figured out by using those two forms, a table of child support awards called the "Schedule of Basic Weekly Child Support Entitlements", and the "Criteria for Deviation from Support Guidelines". An explanation of how to fill out these forms is found at Chapter 10, Section j of this manual.

The guidelines must be used to help judges set the amount of child support in each case. It is not enough to just reach agreement with your spouse on a child support amount.

The guidelines are complicated. You may want to talk to a lawyer about how the guidelines will affect your family's situation. Or, if you are going to use mediation, the court appointed mediators will explain the guidelines and help you complete the forms in mediation. (See Chapter 13 of the divorce book about the mediation process.) However, many judges will also be understanding if you simply cannot figure out how to complete the forms or if your spouse refuses to help.

The guidelines are based on a two step process. First, you must show the incomes of yourself and your spouse on a form called an "Affidavit of Income and Assets". Then, you must apply the formula in the guidelines to that income, to get the "child support obligation", which is the amount of money necessary for each child's needs. This is done on the form called the "Child Support Worksheet".

It is very important for you to provide as much information as possible about your income (and your spouse's income also, if he or she will not be going to the hearing). Pay stubs, income tax returns and bank account statements are all good information for this purpose. If you are able to show the judge enough evidence of your income and your spouse's income, and answer the judge's questions about your family's financial status, this should be enough to allow the judge to set a child support amount.

Once you figure out your family income, you can figure out what the child support amount would be according to the child support tables. An explanation of how to do this is in Chapter 10, section j.

You might decide that the amount from this table isn't fair or doesn't meet your needs. If you do, then try to reach an agreement with your spouse on a different amount. However, whether or not you and your spouse agree on a different amount, the judge will not order it unless you have a good reason. The law lists several reasons that the judge would accept for setting child support differently from the table. This list is reprinted in Appendix II.

If you want a support order that is different from the table, then you should look at the list and be prepared to tell the judge at the hearing why your situation fits one of the reasons in the list.

Income Affidavits and Child Support Worksheets

Maine law requires you and your spouse to each file an Affidavit of Income and Assets. You must also file a Child Support Worksheet together or separately. If your spouse can't or won't file either or both of these forms, you should include as much information as you can about your spouse's income on your own. The Judge will make a decision on the basis of the best information available. These forms **must** be filed within 3 days before the divorce hearing and are discussed in more detail in Chapter 10, Section j.

Tax Considerations

As this book goes to print, child support is not taxable to the spouse receiving it. Under very limited circumstances, the spouse paying child support **may** be entitled to deduct the children on his or her income tax. You may want to consider tax consequences when deciding how to handle this aspect of your divorce. Many times the local office of IRS will answer questions regarding these matters at no cost to you. If they cannot, you may want to consult a lawyer.

Motions Pending Divorce

If you need support before your divorce hearing, then you may want to ask the court to order support to be paid pending the hearing. You can do this by filing a "Motion Pending Divorce" which is described in Chapter 18.

Enforcing Child Support Orders

If an absent parent is not paying support, there are ways to force payment. The law now requires that, in each case where a support order is made, an "Order of Income Withholding" also be made. This order is signed with the Divorce Order and is made a part of it. It gives you the right to have the support withheld from wages or any other source of income of the spouse who owes you child support.

If the Department of Human Services (DHS) has an interest in your divorce (it will if you have been on AFDC or Medicaid or if DHS has agreed to help you collect support), the Order of Income Withholding requires your spouse's employer to withhold support from your spouse's wages. The employer sends the money to DHS even if your spouse is not late in paying support. As this book goes to print, there is no form for this order. The judge or someone from the Department of Human Services should prepare one and attach it to your divorce judgment after the hearing.

If the Department of Human Services is not involved in your divorce, then you must prepare a "Conditional Order of Income Withholding". In order to use this Order after the divorce is final, child support or alimony must be owed for at least one month without payment to you and you must write to your spouse 20 days before serving the Order on his or her employer and include a copy of the Order with that letter. If you meet these conditions, and your spouse does not file a motion in court requesting a "stay" or disputing the amount owed, then you can have the Conditional Order served on your spouse's employer or other source of income. Further instructions on completing and using this form appear in Chapter 10.

There are other ways to force payment as well. You could ask a lawyer to take your ex-spouse back to court; you could ask the Maine Department of Human Services for help; or you could ask for help from your local district attorney.

If, after you have your Divorce Judgment ordering support, your circumstances or your spouse's circumstances change so that the support order is no longer appropriate, then you may ask the Court to change the order. You do this by filing a "Motion to Amend Divorce Judgment", as described in Chapter 19.

e. ALIMONY

Introduction

Alimony is an allowance which a husband or wife must pay, if ordered by the court, to the other spouse for her or his support. It may be ordered paid in a lump sum at the time of the divorce, as periodic payments for a definite or indefinite period of time, or as a nominal amount (e.g., $1.00 per year). The value of an order of alimony for $1.00 per year is that it keeps the issue alive, allowing you to return to court to request more if your circumstances have substantially changed since the divorce decree became final and you now need more. The ex-spouse paying alimony can also ask the judge to reduce alimony based on changed circumstances after the divorce becomes final.

Now or Never

If you are not awarded any alimony in your divorce judgment, you are prohibited by law from returning to court in the future to request it.

How the Court Decides Alimony

Judges will not grant alimony automatically. They will want to know why you are requesting it and will then weigh your reasons and need against your spouse's ability to provide it.

The fault of either party in causing the divorce is not relevant to the award of alimony. The sole purpose of alimony is to provide financial support to a former spouse when necessary.

Courts are required to make alimony decisions based on:

1. The length of the marriage;
2. The ability of each party to pay;
3. The age of each party;
4. The employment history and employment potential of each party;
5. The income history and income potential of each party;
6. The education and training of each party;
7. The provisions for retirement and health insurance benefits of each party;
8. The tax consequences of the division of marital property, including the tax consequences of the sale of the marital home, if applicable;
9. The health and disabilities of each party;
10. The tax consequences of an alimony award;
11. The contributions of either party as homemaker;
12. The contributions of either party to the education or earning potential of the other party;

13. Financial mismanagement by either party resulting in the loss of marital property or income;

14. The standard of living of the parties during the marriage; and

15. Any other factors the court considers appropriate.

A good example of a case in which an order for alimony would be appropriate is the following: a couple has been married for several years. They were immediately married after graduation from high school. He went to work as a salesperson and she stayed at home and raised their family. By the time of their divorce he had been promoted to sales manager, but she had never had any employment experience outside of the home. In this case the court might order alimony to the woman for the period of time necessary for her to make the transition between her roles as a homemaker and a gainfully employed worker.

Many judges are reluctant to order a token amount of alimony. As in all requests for alimony, the judge will want to know that there is good reason for making any order. Some common reasons which may justify a token award of alimony are: illness and the possibility of inability to work and high medical bills in the future; the reasonable belief that transition to employment will not be successful; or a particular vulnerability to cost of living increases.

Tax Considerations

Alimony, unlike child support, is taxable to the spouse receiving it and is a tax deduction for the spouse paying it. You may want to consider tax consequences when deciding how to handle this issue. Many times your local IRS office can answer questions involving this issue at no cost to you. If not, you may want to consult a lawyer.

Nuts and Bolts — Alimony

If you want to request alimony, simply leave the alimony sentence as it is in the prayer section of your Complaint and be prepared to ask for a specific amount at your hearing. It will read:

> "That reasonable alimony, or a specific sum in lieu thereof, be Ordered paid to Plaintiff by Defendant;"

If you do not want alimony, simply cross out this sentence. If you are not sure whether you want to request alimony or not, leave the alimony sentence in. You can withdraw your request at the hearing.

Remember, if you plan to request alimony, be prepared to respond to the judge's concerns with a reasonable and well thought out response, referring to one or more of the 15 reasons listed above.

f. DIVISION OF PROPERTY

Introduction

A married person can own property in two ways. That which is his or hers alone is separate property; that which is owned with his or her spouse is marital property.

In dividing property during a divorce, the judge will first set aside each spouse's separate property to him or her and then divide the marital property between the two.

What Is Marital Property

Property acquired during the marriage is generally considered to be marital property. In fact, the court **presumes** that property acquired during the marriage is marital property no matter whose name it is in or what the agreement was at the time it was purchased. This means that you must prove to the court that something acquired during marriage is **not** marital property.

By statute, marital property does **not** include:

(1) Property acquired by one of the spouses by gift or through inheritance.

(2) Property received during the marriage in exchange for property held by one of the spouses before the marriage. For example, if you owned a home prior to your marriage, sold it and used that money to purchase a new home during your marriage, the new home probably would **not** be considered marital property. However, if the money from the sale of your old home was only enough to make a down payment on the new one, and mortgage payments were made during your marriage, then some of the value of the new home would be marital property and some would not.

(3) Property received during the marriage in exchange for property received by gift or inheritance to one of the spouses.

(4) Property acquired by a spouse **after** a decree of **legal** separation.

(5) Property which both spouses are willing to agree to exclude from the marital property. (This would include property which was the subject of a valid premarital agreement).

(6) The increase in value of property that one spouse owned before the marriage. (For example, if you purchased a piece of land before you were married for $500.00 and during the course of your marriage it increased in value to $5,000.00, the additional value would **not** be considered marital property. The land, now worth $5,000.00 would be your separate property. But, if you used money from a joint bank account to make improvements on the property after your marriage, then some of the increased value would be considered marital property.)

How the Court Divides Property

If you and your spouse cannot agree on how to divide the marital property, then the court is called upon to do the job. The judge will consider the following factors to guide his or her decision:

(1) The contribution of each spouse toward the marital property, including the contribution of the spouse who was the homemaker.

(2) The value of each spouse's non-marital or personal property.

(3) The economic circumstances of each spouse at the time the divorce will be final. The law allows special consideration to be given to the spouse with the children so that they can stay in the family home.

Now or Never

It is very important to consider exactly what kinds of "marital property" exist in your case, and how you would like them to be divided. This is because the divorce judgement regarding the division of marital property is **FINAL. YOU CANNOT GO BACK LATER AND ASK THE COURT TO MAKE CHANGES IN THE WAY PROPERTY WAS DIVIDED** (except in very limited circumstances and these are very difficult to prove. See Chapter 20). In this way, the part of the divorce order regarding marital property is different from the parts regarding parental rights and responsibilities and child support. Earlier in this chapter, it was pointed out that you could ask the court to **modify** a divorce order regarding custody, visitation, child support or alimony (under certain circumstances) if you could show that "circumstances have changed substantially" since the divorce order was final. **BUT,** even if your circumstances do change substantially, you **cannot** ask the court to modify the divorce order regarding marital property.

[**NOTE:** The exception to this rule is when the divorce order doesn't mention something that is marital property. If "marital property" is completely left out of the divorce order, then you can go back to court and ask the judge to re-open the divorce proceeding to include (and divide) this property. However, you can only ask the court to do this for something which was left out of the original order.

If this situation happens to you, you may want to consult a lawyer for advice. In Chapter 20, we have provided sample forms for you to use in court yourself if you want.]

For this reason, it is very important to be sure that you let the court know about all the different kinds of marital property that you and your spouse have acquired. The obvious kinds of marital property include real estate, bank accounts, furniture, automobiles, and appliances. The following things may also be marital property:

— stock certificates and bonds

— military pensions

— other retirement benefits

— the value of a family business

— life insurance

— worker's compensation settlements

If you believe that your spouse may have property that you don't know about, or believe that you cannot get the proper values of the property of which you **are** aware, you definitely should get a lawyer. If you have a great deal of property, or very valuable property, you should also get a lawyer to represent you.

Even if you don't feel that a lawyer is necessary because of the small and uncomplicated nature of your property, you may have to go to court-ordered mediation **if** your spouse does not agree to the division of property that you have proposed **and** you have minor children. The process of court-ordered mediation is discussed in Chapter 13. If you reach this state, you may want to hire a lawyer to represent you at the mediation and/or to negotiate an agreement with your spouse.

Tax Considerations

As in the case of alimony and child support, there may be tax consequences involved in your decision about how to divide the marital property. If this is a concern, once again we recommend that you contact your local IRS office or a lawyer.

Divorce Agreement

However, if you and your spouse are in agreement about how the property should be divided and the agreement is reasonably simple, you may want to do your own divorce agreement. A draft Divorce Agreement is described in Chapter 14. Of course, you can hire a lawyer for the limited purpose of writing the divorce agreement or reviewing the one you have written.

Property List

Whether or not you have made a divorce agreement, Maine law now requires the husband and wife, either together or separately, to file a list of all marital and non-marital property to be divided by the Court and which indicates what property is in dispute. This property list **must** be filed within 3 days before the divorce hearing and is discussed in more detail in Chapter 10, Section i.

Nuts and Bolts — Property

If you want the court to make an order about property, either your own or marital, you will leave as is the printed line in the prayer that reads:

> "That the court set apart to each party his or her property and divide the marital property pursuant to Title 19 M.R.S.A. § 722-A;"

If there is "real property" (land or buildings as opposed to personal property such as cars, furniture and the like) involved in the property settlement, the spouse awarded the real estate must file an abstract of the final divorce decree at the appropriate Registry of Deeds. This procedure will be described more fully in Chapter 17 of this manual.

Again, you should remember that property settlements cannot be changed once a Divorce Judgment is final (except in very limited circumstances and these are difficult to prove. See Chapter 20). If this agreement is not thoughtfully and carefully worked out, one spouse could suffer a serious and permanent loss. If you have questions about marital property it is better to consult an attorney than to risk losing valuable property.

g. BILLS

If there are bills owed by you and your spouse which were accumulated during your marriage, then you will need to decide who will pay them. It is important to understand that orders of the court and agreements between spouses are not legally binding on the people to whom you owe the money.

For example, if before the divorce you owed money to someone, and if the court orders your spouse to pay that bill, and if he or she doesn't pay that bill, then as far as the creditors are concerned you still owe the bill. Your spouse may be in contempt of court if he or she violates the judge's order, but the creditors may still try to get the money from you. (However, you can submit a copy of your divorce judgment which has been "certified" by the court to show your creditors that your spouse was ordered to pay the bill. Sometimes they will then stop trying to collect the bill from you.)

Nuts and Bolts — Bills

You do not have to specifically request payment of outstanding bills in your divorce Complaint. It is considered to be part of the general language in the Prayer which asks:

> "That the Court set apart to each party his or her property and divide the marital property pursuant to Title 19 M.R.S.A. § 722-A."

However, you should be prepared to discuss the status of these outstanding bills at the divorce hearing, if you want the judge to make a specific order regarding them in the divorce judgment. You should bring copies of the bills to court and specifically mention them in your testimony. Or, you may want to include them in any "Divorce Agreement" that you and your spouse sign. (See Chapter 14 for further discussion of Divorce Agreements.)

It is important to remember that these kinds of debts and bills are also "marital property". Once the court makes an order dividing them, that decision is final and can't be changed (except in very limited circumstances and these are difficult to prove. See Chapter 20).

h. RESTORATION OF A PREVIOUS NAME

Upon the request of the wife during the action for divorce or at any time thereafter, the court may change her name. A husband cannot require a wife to change her last name, however. Also, the court is not required to let the wife change her name.

Nuts and Bolts — Name Change

If you want to request that your surname be changed, you will fill in the blank at the end of the printed line in the prayer with the name that you want as follows:

"That the Plaintiff be allowed to change her name to Sally L. Jones;"

You cannot change the last names of your children in a divorce proceeding. If you want to do this, you should contact the County Probate Court for more information.

i. ATTORNEY FEES

You will note that there is a printed request in the prayer that reads:

". . . Reasonable counsel fees be ordered paid by Defendant to
______________________________, Attorney for Plaintiff . . ."

This part of the prayer asks that the court order the Defendant to pay some or all of the Plaintiff's attorney fees. If you are representing yourself, you will probably not have attorney fees and should cross out this printed line. If you do have some attorney's fees for advice or assistance related to your divorce, you can ask the court to order fees payable to your attorney for that help. Just fill in the blank space with the name of your lawyer. The judge will decide whether or not to make this order after looking at the ability to pay of both you and your spouse.

j. HEALTH INSURANCE

There is nothing specific in the prayer section of the Complaint about health insurance. However, many divorce orders make some provision for health insurance.

If you are concerned about this issue (either for yourself or for your children), you may want to ask the judge to include it in the final divorce order. If you are preparing a Divorce Agreement, you may want to include a provision for health insurance in this. The sample "Divorce Agreement" in Chapter 14 has a special section on health insurance.

If your spouse works for an employer who offers health insurance (and employs more than 20 people), you should be able to get that coverage continued for yourself and your children at the group rate, even after the divorce. If you are interested in this option, talk with your spouse's employer or the Consumer Services Division of the Maine Bureau of Insurance in Augusta.

Chapter 7

Dismissal of Previous Divorce Actions

There is one more technical issue you should be aware of before you actually begin your divorce.

If you are certain that neither you nor your spouse has ever filed a divorce action before, involving your present marriage, you do not need to read this chapter. If you are **not certain**, then you should read this chapter very carefully.

If you have ever talked to a lawyer about a divorce from this marriage, or if your spouse has (or even if you think he or she has), you will need to find out whether divorce papers were filed in court.

This is not a difficult task. Simply call the clerk of court in the district where you think the action was started. (Remember, it had to be filed in a court with "venue"; you may want to re-read Chapter 3 discussing venue.) The clerk will check the records and be able to quickly tell you if a previous divorce action has been filed in that court. Be prepared to give the clerk the approximate date when an action might have been filed. If it has been more than 2 years since the divorce was filed, ask the clerk if you can still use these original papers to go forward with your divorce. (**NOTE:** If the divorce action was started in another State by either you or your spouse, consult a lawyer.)

If you have determined that your divorce is active, that is, you have papers pending in Maine court, you have several alternatives:

(1) If YOU Began the Divorce

If you started the divorce, and your spouse did not file a "Counterclaim" also asking for a divorce, then you have the power to stop or continue the divorce action in that court. The Court will tell you if your spouse filed a "Counterclaim." A Counterclaim has the same effect as a Divorce Complaint and allows the person who filed the Counterclaim to go forward and get a divorce even if the original Complaint was dismissed or withdrawn. If he or she did file a counterclaim, then also read the following section entitled "When your spouse started the divorce".

If your Complaint was properly served on your spouse, you may be able to use these papers to get your final Divorce Order. First, you should make sure that the Court still has "venue" over you and your spouse. (That is, that one of you still lives in the area served by that district court.) If the Court still has venue, you can proceed there. If it does not, you will have to dismiss the action, as described below.

Also, if you were represented by a lawyer at that time, you need to decide what to do about the lawyer. If you still want to have the lawyer represent you, you should contact him or her and ask that the divorce proceeding be moved along.

If you no longer want that lawyer to represent you, you should contact him or her and say so. Ask the lawyer to notify the Court that he or she is "withdrawing his or her appearance" as your lawyer. Doublecheck with the Court to make sure that this has been done. If you request it, your lawyer **must** withdraw from the case and cannot insist that you pay him or her first for services to date.

Assuming you have taken care of these matters and are now representing yourself, you can proceed as if you had just filed the Complaint. Just make sure that you have filed all the necessary forms. (See Chapter 10).

(2) If Your SPOUSE Started the Divorce

If your spouse started the divorce by having you served with a Divorce Complaint and Summons, you should check with the Court to see if an Answer or Counterclaim was filed on your behalf. At the same time, you should make sure that the Court has your current address and let them know whether you will be contesting the divorce.

If you did not file a counterclaim then, and don't file one now, it will be completely up to your spouse to proceed or to dismiss the divorce action in that court. You will not have any control over what happens until your spouse takes some action. (Make sure that this court still has "venue" over the case. If it does not have venue and your spouse is insisting on going forward in that court, you should consult an attorney immediately.)

The only way to move a case forward where your spouse started the divorce and is now stalling is by "filing a counterclaim". (This assumes that the court still has "venue".) To file a counterclaim, you can use the same Divorce Complaint form that is available from District Court and fill it out as described in Chapter 10 with two exceptions:

a. Ask the Court Clerk for the docket number of the pending divorce and write that in on the top right side of the form where the words "Docket No." are written; and

b. Cross out "COMPLAINT FOR DIVORCE" and write in "COUNTERCLAIM FOR DIVORCE"

This counterclaim must be served on your spouse as described in Chapter 11. Once it is properly served, you will have the authority to go forward on the divorce complaint, including the right to schedule a hearing as described in Chapter 15.

(3) Dismissing Existing Divorce Actions and Starting Over

There are many reasons why you might prefer to dismiss an existing divorce action and start from scratch. One might be that you and your spouse have moved, and it is more convenient to file your papers and go to a court in your new area. Another might be that a child has been born since the Divorce Complaint was filed. In any case, the spouse who filed the Complaint can dismiss it by writing to the Court. Send a copy of this letter to your lawyer if you were represented in filing that divorce action. The following is a sample letter to the court requesting dismissal of a previous divorce action:

April 8, 1988

Clerk of the Court
Maine District Court
District Eight
Division of Eastern Cumberland

RE: Jane L. Jones v. David D. Jones

Dear Clerk:

Pursuant to Rule 41(a)(1) of the Maine Rules of Civil Procedure, I would like you to dismiss the above-entitled Divorce Action now pending in the Eastern Cumberland District Court, in which I am the plaintiff.

I wish the action to be dismissed without prejudice.

Thank you for your cooperation in this matter.

Sincerely,

Jane L. Jones
Plaintiff

cc: John J. Doe, Esq.
45 Atlantic Street
Brunswick, Maine 01001

REMEMBER: If a counterclaim has been filed, this also must be dismissed by the spouse who filed it. After all pending Complaints and Counterclaims have been dismissed, you can go ahead and file a new Complaint.

Chapter 8

*Divorce For the Battered Spouse**

If your spouse has caused you or your children physical harm, **or** has tried to cause you or your children physical harm, **or** if he has threatened you or the children **or** given you reason to fear that you or the children **may** be harmed, **this is abuse, and you have the right to be protected from it.**

To do this, you request a "Protection from Abuse" Order from the Court. You can do this on an emergency basis, and also ask for an Order which can last up to one year after it is signed by the Court. Both the emergency and the regular Order can include the following:

— an order telling the defendant not to "threaten, assault, molest, harass or otherwise disturb your peace";

— an order telling the defendant not to "impose restraint upon your liberty";

— an order telling the defendant not to enter the family residence or your separate residence;

---

*We will assume that the battered spouse is a woman; in almost all cases, this is true.

- an order concerning the care and custody of your joint minor children, including child support and visitation rights;
- an order that the defendant not take, damage or dispose of property in which you have a legal interest (this includes marital property);
- an order dividing personal property and household goods and furnishings.

IF THE DEFENDANT THEN VIOLATES ANY OF THE ABOVE DESCRIBED ORDERS, HE CAN BE CHARGED WITH A CLASS D CRIME. For many people, the protection which you get from a Protection from Abuse Order is *better* protection than what you get with a final divorce Order, because it is a criminal matter if your ex-spouse then violates any of the conditions of a Protection from Abuse Order.

There is a booklet called "Protection from Abuse — A Guide to Getting a Court Order Without a Lawyer" which explains this process and is available from most libraries, police stations, the offices of Pine Tree Legal Assistance, the Volunteer Lawyer's Project, and shelters for battered spouses. A list of addresses and phone numbers for these shelters is at the end of this chapter. Their staff have a great deal of experience with court and legal advocacy. Getting a Protection from Abuse Order is a simple procedure and should not require a lawyer's help in most cases.

Briefly, these are some things to consider. You may want to get the Protection from Abuse Order **before** serving the Divorce Complaint on your spouse, if there is a possibility that he will abuse you or your children or react in anger to being sued for divorce. For the same reason, you may want to ask the Court to make provision for support and custody and the use of the family home at that time. This Order will govern the relationship between you and your spouse, even after the divorce is filed.

While, in most contested cases involving children, mediation is required, there is an exception to mediation for "extraordinary cause." While the law does not say what "extraordinary cause" is, fear for your safety during mediation, or concern that you may not be able to argue effectively for your rights in the same room with your abuser, is probably "extraordinary cause." This is discussed in more detail in Chapter 13.

Finally, you should **NOT** dismiss your Order for Protection from Abuse when the Divorce Order is signed. As noted above, the Protection from Abuse Order gives you more protection than the Divorce Order with respect to enforcing custody, visitation, freedom from harassment or trespass at the family home, and division of property. Violations of all these terms of the Order are **criminal acts** for which your ex-spouse should be arrested. The only way in which the two Orders offer equal protection is with child support and alimony. Here, a violation of those parts of either the Protection Order or the Divorce Order is only a civil matter and the police cannot get involved.

A Protection from Abuse Order can be "extended" if the defendant continues to abuse you in some way or to violate the terms of the Order. If you want to extend your existing order, check with an attorney or your local Family Crisis shelter for advice at least 30 days prior to the date your order ends.

MEMBER AGENCIES: MAINE COALITION FOR FAMILY CRISIS SERVICES

Abused Women's Advocacy Project
P.O. Box 713
Auburn, Maine 04210
Tel: 795-4020

Abused Women's Advocacy Project
49-50 Main Street
Farmington, Maine 04938
Tel: 778-6107

Family Crisis Shelter
P.O. Box 704
Portland, Maine 04101
Tel: 1-800-537-6066

Ingraham Volunteers
74 Elm Street
Portland, Maine 04102
Tel: 774-HELP (4357)

Family Support Center
P.O. Box 22
Presque Isle, Maine 04769
Tel: 769-8251

Family Support Center
P.O. Box 986
Houlton, Maine 04730
Tel: 532-4004

Family Violence Project
P.O. Box 304
Augusta, Maine 04330
Tel: 623-3569 or
1-800-452-1930 (24 hours/day)

Family Violence Project
P.O. Box 3104
Skowhegan, Maine 04976
Tel: 474-8860

New Hope for Women
P.O. Box 642
Rockland, Maine 04841
Tel: 594-2128

Spruce Run Association
P.O. Box 653
Bangor, Maine 04401
Tel: 947-0496

Spruce Run Association
P.O. Box 524
Ellsworth, Maine 04605
Tel: 667-9489

Womancare/Aegis
P.O. Box 192
Dover-Foxcroft, Maine 04426
Tel: 564-8165 (nights and weekends - Mayo Regional Hospital
564-8401 - ask for a Womancare Assistant)

Womankind
P.O. Box 493
Machias, Maine 04654
Tel: 255-4785

Caring Unlimited
P.O. Box 590
Sanford, Maine 04073
Tel: 282-2182

PART TWO

Mechanics of Obtaining A Maine Divorce

In the preceding pages we have tried to give you some basic information that you will need in deciding whether or not to do your own divorce. You are now ready to begin the divorce process itself. The following pages will explain the procedure step by step. Follow the steps carefully. Accuracy is the single most important thing when it comes to preparing your papers.

The first thing that you will do is purchase the divorce papers themselves . . .

Chapter 9

Pick Up the Papers

You can pick up the papers to begin your divorce from the clerk of the Civil Division of any Maine District Court. Usually it will be easiest to go to the court serving the town where you live. To find out which court that is, match up the city or town where you live with the corresponding court in the Court and County Locator in the Appendix of this manual.

The following is a list of papers that you will need to purchase at the court. We suggest you buy two originals of each form so that you will have a spare in case you make a mistake.

Everyone needs the following:

* Divorce Complaint;
* Divorce Summons;
* Federal Affidavit; and
* Property List (not every court will have one, but you should be sure to ask).

If you have children from this marriage you will also need:

* Uniform Child Custody Jurisdiction Act Affidavit;
* 2 Affidavits of Income and Assets; 1 Child Support Worksheet; and
* Conditional Order of Income Withholding.

You may also need:

* Affidavit and Application to Proceed In Forma Pauperis if you don't have money to pay the court fees and sheriff's cost. (See Chapter 10);

and

* A Conditional Order of Income Withholding if alimony will be ordered in your case (and you have not already purchased one for Child Support).

Chapter 10

Fill Out the Papers

a. INTRODUCTION

In the sections that follow you will be given step by step instructions on how to fill out the necessary court papers. There are sample forms included together with an explanation of the forms and detailed instructions on how to fill them out.

It may be tempting to pick up this book and begin here, without reading Chapters 1 through 8 first. Please don't. The information in those chapters is important and you need it in order to fill these forms out correctly. Chapter 6 is especially important.

With a typewriter, carefully complete each form neatly and exactly as shown. If you don't have a typewriter and can't use somebody else's, the court may accept handwritten papers if they are printed neatly in ink.

You will need to prepare an original of each form. Make two copies. Generally speaking, one will be given to your spouse and you will keep one for yourself. You should also keep copies of all letters you send in connection with your divorce.

These forms may change somewhat in the future, but the information in this manual should make it possible for you to fill out any forms accurately.

There are some things you must learn that apply to all forms:

1. **Plaintiff/Defendant:** You (assuming that you are the person starting the divorce) are the "Plaintiff". Your spouse is the "Defendant".

2. **Names:** You must use your full, married name on these forms. Be consistent. Names should always appear exactly the same way each time (including signatures). Your "married name" is the name you used uniformly after your marriage on papers and legal documents. If you kept your birth name after your marriage, that would be your married name.

3. **Who gets what paper:** The court always gets the original of each form, the Defendant gets a copy, and you keep one for your files.

4. **Abbreviations:** You should not abbreviate when filling out the forms. For example, write "Maine", not "Me."

b. THE DIVORCE COMPLAINT

The Divorce Complaint is a form that states the basic facts about your marriage and tells the court what you are asking for once the marriage is dissolved. The Complaint is served on your spouse so he or she will know what you are requesting.

You will need to prepare one Divorce Complaint. The original form should be filed with the court, and you should make one copy for your spouse, and one copy for your files. Be sure that the form is completed neatly.

Our instructions are designed to cover a broad range of circumstances, so be sure to fill out your own forms only as the instructions apply to you. You may want to re-read Chapter 6 at this time. It discusses each "prayer" or request, that you may want to make to the court. You may want to begin by looking at the blank Complaint in the Appendix and compare this with the completed sample Complaint, which is Form 1 in this Chapter.

Each number printed on the form Complaint for Divorce is considered a new paragraph. The following discussion of how to fill out the Complaint is organized by those paragraphs. It starts from the top of the form and works through it to the end.

STATE OF MAINE

District Court
Division of Eastern Cumberland
Location Brunswick, Maine
Docket No. ____________

SUSAN T. BROWN Plaintiff

vs.

COMPLAINT FOR DIVORCE

JOHN D. BROWN Defendant

1. Plaintiff was lawfully married to John D. Brown at Freeport in the County of Cumberland and State of Maine on the 14th day of July, 1969.

2. Plaintiff resides in [town or city] Freeport, [State] Maine.

3. (Defendant resides in [town or city] Bar Harbor, [State] Maine.)
~~(The residence of Defendant is unknown to Plaintiff and cannot be ascertained by reasonable diligence.)~~
[Delete statement that does not apply. If residence of Defendant is unknown, complete the affidavit on the reverse side.]

4. This court has jurisdiction because (check the following statements that are applicable):
[X] A. Plaintiff has resided in this State in good faith for six months prior to the commencement of this action;
[X] B. Plaintiff is a resident of this State and the parties were married in this State;
[X] C. Plaintiff is a resident of this State and the parties resided in this State when the cause of action accrued;
[X] D. Defendant is a resident of this State;

5. The only other divorce or annulment actions previously commenced between the parties, together with the designation of the court or courts involved and the disposition thereof, are as follows:
Divorce action in District Court of Eastern Cumberland was dismissed without prejudice on April 19, 1972

6. There is real and personal property of the parties as defined by 19 M.R.S.A. § 722-A, as amended;

7. Plaintiff asserts the following grounds for divorce (check the applicable ground):
[X] A. Irreconcilable marital differences exist between the parties;
[ ] B. Defendant has been guilty of cruel and abusive treatment towards Plaintiff;
[ ] C. Other ____________.

8. The following child(ren) have been born to the parties (list children including date of birth):
Margaret Alexandria Brown (d/o/b April 1, 1980); Nathan Johnathan Brown (d/o/b November 9, 1982); Sally Janice Brown (d/o/b May 5, 1983)*
An affidavit concerning child custody is attached hereto. *Check one of the following:*
[ ] A. (Plaintiff) (Defendant) is receiving, has received or will be receiving public assistance for the above child(ren).
[X] B. No one is receiving, has received or will be receiving public assistance for the above child(ren).

9. There is no collusion between Plaintiff and Defendant to obtain a divorce.

*Mary Penelope Brown (d/o/b October 10, 1987)

DCCV 14 Rev. (11/86)

WHEREFORE, Plaintiff prays that a divorce from the bonds of matrimony between Plaintiff and Defendant be adjudged;

That the parental rights and responsibilities regarding the minor child(ren), including child support payments, be determined;

That the Court set apart to each party his or her property and divide the marital property pursuant to Title 19, M.R.S.A. § 722-A;

~~That reasonable alimony, or a specific sum in lieu thereof, be ordered paid to Plaintiff by Defendant;~~ --

~~That reasonable counsel fees be ordered paid by Defendant to~~------ __________
~~Attorney for Plaintiff, execution to issue therefor when decree of divorce is granted; and~~

That Plaintiff be allowed to change her name to Susan Temple.

Dated at Freeport, Maine, this 3rd day of July, 19 90.

By: __________ Susan T. Brown
~~(Attorney for) Plaintiff~~ Plaintiff Susan T. Brown Pro Se

Back Road
Address

Freeport, Maine 04032

865-6000
Telephone

****

STATE OF MAINE

__________ County

Personally appeared __________ above named Plaintiff and made Oath that the foregoing allegation as to the residence of the Defendant is true.

Before me,

____
Notary Public / Attorney at Law

The Caption

This is the information that tells the Court Clerk how to file your Complaint. Every form you file with the Court should have the same information, written in the same way, on the caption, except for the name of the form you are filing. Example:

STATE OF MAINE

District Court
Division of Eastern Cumberland [A]
Location Brunswick, Maine [B]
Docket No. ______ [C]

[D] SUSAN T. BROWN Plaintiff

vs. **COMPLAINT FOR DIVORCE** [F]

[E] JOHN D. BROWN Defendant

A. Division of the court where you are bringing the action. Refer to the Court and County Locator at the end of this manual.

B. The town and state where the court is physically located.

C. Leave the Civil Action Docket Number blank.

D. Your full name before the word Plaintiff.

E. Your spouse's full name before the word Defendant.

F. The name of the "form". This will be printed on the form when you purchase it from the Court.

Jurisdiction

The first four paragraphs of the Complaint for Divorce show that the court has jurisdiction and venue over your case. (You may want to re-read Chapter 3 to refresh your memory of these points.) Example:

1. Plaintiff was lawfully married to John D. Brown [A] at Freeport [B] in the County of Cumberland [C] and State of Maine [D] on the 14th [E] day of July [F], 19 69 [G].

2. Plaintiff resides in [town or city] Freeport [H], [State] Maine [I].

3. (Defendant resides in [town or city] Bar Harbor [J], [State] Maine [K].)
(~~The residence of Defendant is unknown to Plaintiff and cannot be ascertained by reasonable diligence.~~)
[Delete statement that does not apply. If residence of Defendant is unknown, complete the affidavit on the reverse side.]

4. This court has jurisdiction because (check the following statements that are applicable): [L]
[X] A. Plaintiff has resided in this State in good faith for six months prior to the commencement of this action;
[X] B. Plaintiff is a resident of this State and the parties were married in this State;
[X] C. Plaintiff is a resident of this State and the parties resided in this State when the cause of action accrued;
[X] D. Defendant is a resident of this State;

A. Your spouse's full name, exactly as it appears above.

B. The town where the marriage took place.

C. The County where the marriage took place.

D. The State where the marriage took place.

E. The day on which you were married.

F. The month in which you were married.

G. The year in which you were married.

H. The town where you presently are living.

I. The State where you presently are living.

J. The town where your spouse is presently living.

K. The State where your spouse is presently living.

L. Finally, the form indicates you should place a check or an "X" beside each statement which is true. In order for the Court to have jurisdiction, at least one statement must be true. It is all right to put a check or "X" beside several or all of the statements, if most or all of them are true.

NOTE: If you don't know where your spouse is living, cross out the top line in paragraph #3 of the Complaint. If you do know where he/she is living, cross out the second line in paragraph #3, and fill in the appropriate city/town and state.

Dismissal of Previous Actions

You should re-read Chapter 7 on previous divorce actions that either you or your spouse have filed regarding this marriage. This is why Paragraph 5 is included on the Complaint for Divorce. Example:

5. The only other divorce or annulment actions previously commenced between the parties, together with the designation of the court or courts involved and the disposition thereof, are as follows:
   Divorce action in District Court in Brunswick was dismissed
   without prejudice on April 19, 1972 [A]

A. If **no** previous divorce actions have been filed in your case, write "none" on the line. If a previous divorce action was filed, you should write down the address of the district court in which it was filed and what happened to the case (see **[A]** above). (Was it dismissed, was it denied, etc.) For instance, if a divorce action was filed in 1983 in District Court in Augusta and you dismissed it, you would write **"District Court in Augusta, Maine in 1983 - it was dismissed".**

Marital Property

Paragraph 6 of the Complaint tells the Court that there is marital property of some kind. You may want to re-read Chapter 6 on marital and personal property to refresh your memory of what marital property is. Example:

6. There is real and personal property of the parties as defined by 19 M.R.S.A. § 722-A, as amended;

It is much safer to leave this sentence in, even if you are not sure whether you have marital property. You should only cross this sentence out if you are absolutely sure that you and your spouse have no marital property at all. However, you should cross out the words "real and" if you and your spouse don't own any land or buildings.

Grounds for Divorce

Paragraph 7 of the Complaint tells the Court why you are filing for divorce. You should re-read Chapter 4 if you have questions. Example:

7. Plaintiff asserts the following grounds for divorce (check the applicable ground):
   [X] A. Irreconcilable marital differences exist between the parties;
   [ ] B. Defendant has been guilty of cruel and abusive treatment towards Plaintiff;
   [ ] C. Other ______________________________

Check whichever ground applies. Although most people check only one ground, you may check more than one if you want. If you plan to check both "irreconcilable marital differences" and "cruel and abusive treatment", re-read Chapter 4, Section b. If the basis for your divorce is not either "irreconcilable marital differences" or "cruel and abusive treatment", then you should check (C) and type in the actual name of the ground from the list in Chapter 4, after "Other". But, if you are considering checking (C), you should re-read Chapter 4 and probably talk with a lawyer first.

Children of the Marriage

Paragraph 8 of the Complaint is a list of all your living children over which you have legal custody or guardianship with your spouse. As a general rule, you should list natural children of you and your spouse which were born before and after the marriage, as well as children which have been adopted by you and your spouse. Example:

8. The following child(ren) have been born to the parties (list children including date of birth):
   Margaret Alexandria Brown (d/o/b April 1, 1980); Nathan Johnathan Brown (d/o/b November 9, 1982); Sally Janice Brown (d/o/b May 5, 1983)*
   An affidavit concerning child custody is attached hereto. *Check one of the following:*
   [ ] A. (Plaintiff) (Defendant) is receiving, has received or will be receiving public assistance for the above child(ren).
   [X] B. No one is receiving, has received or will be receiving public assistance for the above child(ren).

9. There is no collusion between Plaintiff and Defendant to obtain a divorce.

*Mary Penelope Brown (d/o/b October 10, 1987)

DCCV 14 Rev. (11/86)

You should write out each child's full legal name and his or her date of birth on the lines provided in the Complaint. If there is not enough space to list your children, you should place an * at the end of the second blank line, and then list the remaining children at the bottom of the first page of the Complaint, as in the sample Complaint (Form1).

Public Assistance

The second part of Paragraph 8 is intended to identify whether either you or your spouse are now receiving, have received, or will be receiving public assistance for the children you have listed in Paragraph 8. You may want to re-read the section on "Child Support" in Chapter 6 before completing this Paragraph. Example:

An affidavit concerning child custody is attached hereto. *Check one of the following:*
[ ] A. (Plaintiff) (Defendant) is receiving, has received or will be receiving public assistance for the above child(ren).
[x] B. No one is receiving, has received or will be receiving public assistance for the above child(ren).

Place a check beside **[A.]** if you, as Plaintiff, are or will be receiving public assistance for the children, you should also cross out the word (Defendant) in that line. If your spouse is or will be receiving public assistance for the children, you should cross out the word (Plaintiff) in that line.

Otherwise, you should check **[B.]** to indicate that neither you nor your spouse has, is or will be receiving public assistance for the children. As used here, "public assistance" means AFDC, Medicaid, or State Supplemental SSI.

Collusion

Paragraph 9 of the Complaint is a statement that you and your spouse have not colluded to obtain this divorce. You may want to re-read Chapter 5 to refresh your memory on what collusion is. Remember, you cannot get a divorce if you and your spouse have colluded to obtain it. Therefore, you should never cross out this sentence.

Prayer for Relief

The first page of the Divorce Complaint contains all the factual statements which show why the Court has jurisdiction over your divorce and why a divorce should be granted. It also tells the Court about everything that the Court might be required to include in the final Divorce Order: children, marital property and child support payments to one spouse or the Department of Human Services.

The back side of the Complaint for Divorce is called the "Prayer". It starts with the word "**WHEREFORE.**" This is the section where you, as Plaintiff, tell the Court what you would like the Court to do in its final Divorce Order.

You no longer have to specifically tell the Court, on the Complaint form itself, what kind of custody arrangement you want, or that you want to divide the marital property in a particular way. You should, however, cross out any sentences in the "Prayer" that do not apply to you. Example:

WHEREFORE, Plaintiff prays that a divorce from the bonds of matrimony between Plaintiff and Defendant be adjudged;

That the parental rights and responsibilities regarding the minor child(ren), including child support payments, be determined; [A]

That the Court set apart to each party his or her property and divide the marital property pursuant to Title 19, M.R.S.A. § 722-A; [B]

~~That reasonable alimony, or a specific sum in lieu thereof, be ordered paid to Plaintiff by Defendant;~~ [C]

~~That reasonable counsel fees be ordered paid by Defendant to~~ ______________ [D]
~~Attorney for Plaintiff, execution to issue therefor when decree of divorce is granted; and~~

That Plaintiff be allowed to change her name to Susan Temple [E]

Dated at Freeport [F], Maine, this 3 [G] day of July [H], 19 88. [I]

By: ______________________
~~(Attorney for) Plaintiff~~ [J]

Susan T. Brown [K]
Plaintiff Susan T. Brown Pro Se

Back Road [L]
Address

Freeport, Maine 04032

865-4499
Telephone

Explanation of above:

(A) If you don't have any children from this marriage, you should cross out line A. If you do have children from this marriage, leave it in. This line will be the basis for your custody, child support and visitation order.

(B) If you don't have any marital property, you should cross out line B, but remember that most people do have marital property and it is safer to leave this line in.

(C) If you don't want alimony, cross out line C.

(D) Normally, since you are representing yourself, you would cross out line D. However, if you had to consult an attorney at some point in connection with this divorce, leave this line in.

(E) If you are a woman who wants to stop using her current married name and change your last name to something else, you should write in your preferred full name here. Otherwise, you should cross this line E out.

(F) You should write in the town where you live.

(G) The day of the month you sign the Complaint.

(H) The month you sign the Complaint.

(I) The year you sign the Complaint.

(J) Since you are representing yourself, you should cross out (Attorney for) Plaintiff.

(K) You should sign your name on this line. Underneath it, you should print your name and the words "pro se".

(L) Your address and phone number.

Make sure all the information is correct and that the Court can read the information. If you have made mistakes and crossed out things without meaning to do that, **start over.**

NOTE: You do **not** have to sign this Complaint in front of a Notary Public or fill out the very bottom section of the form referring to the residence of your spouse, **except** when you don't know where your spouse is living and you have to make service by publication. See Chapter 11.

c. THE DIVORCE SUMMONS

The Divorce Summons is a legal message from you to the Defendant (your spouse) telling him or her that a Complaint has been filed which concerns him or her. It also tells your spouse that if there is no written response (an Answer) from either him or her within twenty days, the court may go ahead and grant you what you have asked for in the Complaint. A copy of the Complaint and Summons must be served on the Defendant.

The Summons is quite simple to fill out. Carefully complete the form neatly and exactly as shown in the following instructions. Be sure to use the form of your name that you used in the Complaint. For example, if you used "Susan T. Brown" in the Complaint, be sure that it appears that way in the Summons too.

Before filling out the Summons, check to make certain that the **current** clerk of court has signed (or stamped) his or her name on it. You can call the District Court where you got the Summons to make sure. Also be sure that he or she has impressed his or her seal on the Summons.

You will need an original and 2 copies of the Divorce Summons. One copy will be given to your spouse when service is made and the sheriff will write on the original. You will then need to give the original Summons to the Court. You should keep one copy for your files.

Again, we suggest you begin by looking first at the blank Summons in the Appendix and comparing it with a sample completed Summons which is Form 2 in this Chapter.

Completing the Divorce Summons

Refer to the sample completed Form 2 to see where the corresponding letters appear.

A through E should be written exactly as they appear on the Complaint for Divorce.

F. The name of the form. This will be printed on the form

G. Type in your spouse's name and full address. It is better to use a street address, if you know what that is, instead of a mailing address.

H. Your name.

I. Where the District Court is located.

J. The County where the District Court is located.

K. The street address for the District Court.

L. The town where the District Court is located.

M. The date you signed the Summons.

N. Your signature, address and phone number. (Cross out "Attorney for" and add "Pro se".)

O. Leave this blank. The sheriff fills this in after service has been made on your spouse.

You do not write anything on the back side of the Divorce Summons. The Sheriff will fill in all this information when the Complaint and Summons are served on your spouse. Chapter 11 has an explanation of *how* to have your spouse served.

FORM 2

STATE OF MAINE

(Seal of the Court)

District Court
Division of Eastern Cumberland [A]
Location Brunswick, Maine [B]
Docket No. ______________ [C]

[D] SUSAN T. BROWN Plaintiff

vs.

[E] JOHN D. BROWN Defendant

DIVORCE SUMMONS

To the Defendant John D. Brown [G]
Address: 15 Main Street
Bar Harbor, Maine 04609

The Plaintiff Susan T. Brown [H] has begun a lawsuit against you in the District Court which holds sessions at Brunswick [I] in Cumberland [J] County. If you wish to oppose the divorce, you or your attorney MUST FILE A WRITTEN ANSWER to the attached Complaint within 20 days from the day this Summons was served upon you. You or your attorney must file your Answer by delivering it in person or by mail to the office of the Clerk of the District Court, 10 Federal [K] Street, Brunswick [L] Maine. On or before the day you file your Answer, you or your attorney must mail a copy of your Answer to the (Attorney for) Plaintiff, whose address appears below.

IMPORTANT WARNING: IF YOU FAIL TO FILE AN ANSWER WITHIN THE TIME STATED ABOVE, OR IF YOU FAIL TO APPEAR AT ANY TIME THE COURT NOTIFIES YOU TO DO SO, A JUDGMENT BY DEFAULT MAY BE ENTERED AGAINST YOU IN YOUR ABSENCE FOR THE DIVORCE AND ANY OTHER RELIEF DEMANDED.

IF YOU DO NOT FILE AN ANSWER, BUT YOU WISH TO BE ADVISED OF THE DATE OF HEARING OR TO BE HEARD ON PARENTAL RIGHTS OF CHILDREN, ALIMONY, SUPPORT, COUNSEL FEES OR DIVISION OF PROPERTY YOU SHOULD NOTIFY THE CLERK IN WRITING.

IF AN ORDER FOR PAYMENT OF MONEY IS ENTERED AGAINST YOU, YOUR EMPLOYER MAY BE ORDERED TO PAY PART OF YOUR WAGES TO THE PLAINTIFF OR YOUR PERSONAL PROPERTY, INCLUDING BANK ACCOUNTS, AND YOUR REAL ESTATE MAY BE TAKEN TO SATISFY THE JUDGMENT.

IF YOU INTEND TO OPPOSE THE DIVORCE, **DO NOT FAIL TO ANSWER WITHIN THE REQUIRED TIME.**

If you believe you have a defense to the Plaintiff's Complaint or if you believe you have a claim of your own against the Plaintiff, you may wish to talk to a lawyer. If you feel you cannot afford to pay a fee to a lawyer, you may ask a Clerk of the District Court for information as to places where you may seek legal assistance.

Dated: July 3, 1988 [M]

Susan T. Brown [N]
(~~Attorney for~~) Plaintiff
Pro Se

Back Road, Freeport, Maine 04032
Address

(207) 865-6000
Telephone

This Summons is issued by:
Shane A. Burns
Clerk of the District Court

Division of ______________ [O]

Served on ______________
(Date)

____
Deputy Sheriff

DCCV-2 Rev. (5/85)

d. FEDERAL AFFIDAVIT

The Federal Affidavit is a form which you will purchase from the court clerk, complete, and return to the court **on the day of your divorce hearing**. Its purpose is to tell the judge that your spouse is not in the military service. Spouses in the military service have special legal protections under the Soldiers and Sailors Civil Relief Act. The procedure for divorcing a military spouse is described in Chapter 11 of this manual.

Everyone whose spouse is **not** in the military service must file a Federal Affidavit.

Most courts require you to prepare, sign, and have the form notarized as close as possible to the day of the divorce hearing so that they will have the most timely information. This form does not have to be served on your spouse. Check with your local court clerk to learn what the procedure for filing the Federal Affidavit is in your locality. Also ask if the Clerk will notarize it for you on the day of the hearing.

Once again, a blank Federal Affidavit is in the Appendix and a sample completed Affidavit appears here as Form 3.

Instructions on Completing the Federal Affidavit

Remember, this information should be current on the day of your hearing. For that reason, you should wait to fill out this form until the day of your hearing is only one or two days away. The letters below refer to the letters which appear on Form 3.

A. The County in which the District Court is located.

B. The Division of the District Court.

C. The location of the District Court by town and State.

D. Leave the civil docket number blank.

E. Your full name.

F. Your spouse's full name.

G. Your full name.

H. Since you are representing yourself, you should cross out everything (i.e., "or____________________________attorney of record for the Plaintiff in the above-entitled action") up to the words "on Oath, etc."

I. This is a statement of where your spouse is living and working, to the best of your knowledge. If he or she is not working, just say that.

J. Your spouse's full name.

K. Leave blank.

L. This is a statement of residence of either you or the Defendant in a particular town and County in Maine, to show that the District Court has "venue." (You may want to re-read Chapter 3 again.)

M. You should sign the Affidavit on this line. Cross out "Attorney for" and type your full name after Plaintiff with the words "Pro se" at the end. Do not sign until you are in the presence of a notary public.

N. The notary will complete the bottom portion of the Affidavit.

FORM 3

FEDERAL AFFIDAVIT

STATE OF MAINE

[A] CUMBERLAND County
(Indicate County Where Issued)

District Court
Division of Eastern Cumberland [B]
Location Brunswick, Maine [C]
Docket Number ______________ [D]

[E] SUSAN T. BROWN

Plaintiff

vs.

FEDERAL AFFIDAVIT

[F] JOHN D. BROWN

Defendant

I, Susan T. Brown [G] Plaintiff, ~~or~~ ______________ [H]
~~attorney of record for the Plaintiff in the above entitled action~~, on Oath depose and say on my own knowledge, that the Defendant is a resident of Bar Harbor, Maine and is employed
[I] at the Hacock Fish Factory.

(Facts, i.e.: Residence, Employment, etc.)

And at this date the said Defendant John D. Brown [J] is not in the Military Service of the United States, as defined in Article I of the "Soldiers' and Sailors' Relief Act of 1940," as amended.

[K] ______________

(Facts as to residence of Plaintiff or Defendant or place of service of process, etc.)

AND FURTHER REPRESENTS the Affiant under Oath that the facts showing that venue was properly laid at the place where this action was brought are as follows:

[L] Plaintiff is a resident of Freeport, Maine

Susan T. Brown [M]
~~(Attorney for)~~ Plaintiff
Pro Se

STATE OF MAINE

______________ County ______________, 19____

[N] Personally appeared the above-named ______________
and made Oath that the foregoing Affidavit by him/her is true.

Before me, ______________
Notary Public/Attorney at Law

DCCV-22 Rev. (1/83)

e. AFFIDAVIT & APPLICATION TO PROCEED IN FORMA PAUPERIS

If you are financially unable to pay for the court fees, including the Sheriff's charges for serving the Complaint [and the $60 mediation fee, if that becomes necessary], you should file this Affidavit with your Complaint. As a general rule, if your expenses for basic necessities are greater than the income you receive in a normal month, you should file an Affidavit **In Forma Pauperis**, that is a request to proceed without cost to you.

A blank sample form is in the Appendix and a sample completed Affidavit appears here as Form 4.

Instructions on Completing the Affidavit

Again, these letters correspond to those letters which appear on Form 4.

A through E should contain the same information that appears on the caption of every other form filed in connection with your divorce.

F. Your full name.

G. Add the words "and mediation fee" at the end of the first line of paragraph 1 as shown.

H. Your average total monthly income after taxes.

I. Your average total monthly expenses for basic necessities (food, shelter, heat, lights, etc.)

J. The date you are signing this Affidavit.

K. Your signature. **BE SURE TO SIGN IN THE PRESENCE OF A NOTARY PUBLIC OR ATTORNEY.**

L. The **Notary** will sign the form here.

M. Type in the words "It is ordered that any mediation fee is waived" here.

N. The **Judge** will date and sign the form here.

FORM 4

STATE OF MAINE

SUPERIOR COURT
______________, ss.
Docket No. ______________

DISTRICT COURT
Division of Eastern Cumberland [A]
Location Brunswick, Maine [B]
Docket No. ______________ [C]

[D] SUSAN T. BROWN

Plaintiff

vs.

[E] JOHN D. BROWN

Defendant

AFFIDAVIT AND APPLICATION TO PROCEED IN FORMA PAUPERIS

I, Susan T. Brown [F], request leave of court to proceed in forma pauperis.

1. I am without the funds to pay the filing fee, ~~and~~ service costs, and mediation fee. [G]

   My monthly income is $ 1, 400. [H]

   My necessary monthly expenses are $ 1,400. [I]

2. I possess no other source from which the filing or service fees can be paid.

3. I bring this action or defense in good faith.

4. I agree to reimburse any fee or service costs which have been waived or paid if at any time during the pendency of the action I am financially able to do so.

Dated: July 3, 1988 [J]

Susan T. Brown [K]

Personally appeared the above named affiant, and made oath, to the truth of the foregoing affidavit, signed before me.

L]

Dated: July 3, 1988

Jane S. Smith
Notary Public/~~Attorney~~

ORDER

The court finds that the above named affiant is proceeding in good faith and is without sufficient funds to pay the filing fee, service costs or removal fee.

It is ORDERED that the filing (removal) fee is waived.
M] It is ORDERED that any mediation fee is waived.
It is ORDERED that the service costs be paid as an administrative expense.

N] Dated: July 5, 1988

Kate S. Abbott
Judge, District Court
~~Justice, Superior Court~~

SC-2/DCCV-4 (1/86)
CV-34 (1/86)

f. UNIFORM CHILD CUSTODY JURISDICTION ACT AFFIDAVIT

If you listed any children in Paragraph 8 of the Complaint for Divorce, you must file a Uniform Child Custody Jurisdiction Act Affidavit with your Divorce Complaint.

Instructions on Completion of the UCCJA Affidavit

Again, a blank Affidavit is contained in the Appendix and the sample completed Affidavit follows in this chapter as Form 5. The letters below refer to the letters which appear on Form 5.

A through E should be completed in the same way they appear in the caption of the other forms you are filing with the Court.

F. Your children's names and dates of birth should be listed here exactly as they appear in Paragraph 8 of the Complaint for Divorce.

G. Where your children are physically living at the time you sign this Affidavit. This may be your address, your spouse's address, or some other person's address. However, temporary visits to another address don't count. Instead, you should write down the address for the place the children consider "home".

H. As the form requests, you should list all the places that your children have lived within the last 5 years, together with the time that they lived at each address and the name and current address of the person(s) with whom they lived at that time. It does not matter whether you start with their addresses five years ago, or their current address, so long as the entire five year period is covered. (See the sample form for examples.)

I. If you have participated as a party or witness in any litigation affecting the custody of these children, you should consult with a lawyer before completing this form. If not, you should cross out the words "except as follows".

J. If you are aware of someone, other than your spouse, who has physical custody of the children or who claims to have custody or visiting rights of some kind, you should consult a lawyer before completing this form. If not, you should cross out the words "except as follows".

K. This is for your signature and address. **BE SURE TO SIGN THIS AFFIDAVIT IN THE PRESENCE OF A NOTARY PUBLIC.**

L. The Notary will fill this section out.

FORM 5

STATE OF MAINE

SUPERIOR COURT
______________________, ss.
Docket No.______________

DISTRICT COURT
Division of Eastern Cumberland [A]
Location Brunswick, Maine [B]
Docket No. ______________ [C]

[D] SUSAN T. BROWN Plaintiff

vs.

[E] JOHN D. BROWN Defendant

AFFIDAVIT
CONCERNING CHILD CUSTODY
(TITLE 19, M.R.S.A. SEC. 810)

1. This proceeding involves a request for the court to determine the custody of

[F]
Mary P. Brown Date of Birth October 10, 1987
Nathan J. Brown Date of Birth November 9, 1982
Sally J. Brown Date of Birth May 5, 1983
Margaret A. Brown Date of Birth April 1, 1980

[G] 2. The present address of said child(ren) is Back Road, Freeport, Maine 04032

3. The following is a complete list of the places where said child(ren) have lived within the past five years, and the names and *present address* of all persons with whom said child(ren) have lived during that period:

	Dates of Residence	Place (City and State)	Person with whom child(ren) have lived: Name	Present Address
[H]	1985-1988	Freeport, Maine	Susan T. Brown and John D. Brown	Back Road Freeport, Maine 04032 15 Main Street Bar Harbor, Maine 04609
	1983-1985	Augusta, Maine	Susan T. Brown and John D. Brown	Back Road Freeport, Maine 04032 15 Main Street Bar Harbor, Maine 04609

[I] 4. The undersigned has not participated as a party, witness or in any other capacity in other litigation concerning the custody of said child(ren), in this or any other State, ~~except as follows:~~

THE UNDERSIGNED WILL ADVISE THE COURT OF ANY SUCH HEARING ARISING HEREAFTER.

DCCV-35 Rev. (1/86)
CV-40 (1/86)

[J] 5. There is no person, not a party to the present proceeding, who has physical custody of said child(ren), or claims to have custody or visiting rights with respect to said child(ren), ~~except as follows:~~ ______

______

______

______

______

The undersigned under oath and subject to the penalties of perjury, hereby declares that the statements made herein are true, upon the personal knowledge, information and belief of the undersigned, and so far as upon information and belief, that the undersigned believes them to be true.

[K] Signed *Susan T Brown*

Address Back Road

Freeport, Maine 04032

STATE OF MAINE

CUMBERLAND County

[L] Personally appeared the above named Susan T. Brown and signed and made oath to the foregoing affidavit, before me,

Dated July 3, 1988

Jane Smith

Notary Public/~~Attorney at Law~~

g. CERTIFICATE OF NOTICE

If you or your spouse have, are now or will be likely to receive public assistance for your children, you will be required to give notice of your Divorce Complaint to the Department of Human Services. Many courts require proof that you have done this and want you to file a formal "Certificate of Notice" which says so.

A sample completed "Certificate of Notice" follows as Form 6. A blank copy of the "Certificate of Notice" is provided in the Appendix.

Instructions on Completing Certificate of Notice

The letters below correspond to letters on the sample completed Form 6.

A through E will be the same information as on the Complaint and other forms.

F. Your name.

G. Your name.

H. Your spouse's name.

I. The date on which you mailed a copy of the Divorce Complaint to Department of Human Services.

J. Your signature.

FORM 6 -- CERTIFICATE OF NOTICE

STATE OF MAINE

DISTRICT COURT
Division of Eastern Cumberland [A]
Location Brunswick [B]
Docket No.____________________ [C]

* * * * * * * * * * * * * * *
[D] SUSAN T. BROWN, Plaintiff *
*
-vs- * CERTIFICATE OF NOTICE
*
[E] JOHN D. BROWN, Defendant *
* * * * * * * * * * * * * * *

Pursuant to 19 M.R.S.A. § 776(3), in any action to establish or enforce a Support Order, when a minor child has received, or is receiving public assistance, the party must send a copy of the Motion or Petition to the Department of Human Services.

The Plaintiff, Susan T. Brown [F] , hereby certifies that ~~he~~/she sent on this day by, ordinary mail, a copy of a Complaint for Divorce, being filed with this Court in the case of Susan T. Brown [G] vs. John D. Brown [H] to the Department of Human Services at the following address:

Central Office Supervisor
Division of Support Enforcement
Department of Human Services
State House Station #11
Augusta, Maine 04333

Dated: July 5, 1988 [I]

Susan T. Brown [J]

h. CONDITIONAL ORDER OF INCOME WITHHOLDING

Maine law now requires every divorce order to provide for automatic income withholding **when child support or alimony is part of the order**. The easiest way to meet this requirement is by getting a form "Conditional Order of Income Withholding" from the court with your other forms.

Bring this form with you to court on the day of the hearing. This Order will be signed by the judge at the hearing and becomes part of the total divorce order. You can use this Order when your ex-spouse owes you an amount equal to one month's worth of child support or alimony.

After this Order has been signed, you may use it by first writing to your ex-spouse, including a copy of the Order, and telling him or her the amount you believe is owed. Be sure to make a copy of this letter. It may be helpful to send it by certified mail, so you can prove that he/she got it.

You must write to your ex-spouse at least 20 days *before* you write to his or her employer. The letter to the employer should include a copy of the Order and a statement telling the employer how much money is owed. You must send a copy of this letter to the Department of Human Services at the following address:

Central Office Supervisor
Division of Support Enforcement
Department of Human Services
State House Station #11
Augusta, Maine 04333

As long as your ex-spouse has not filed a motion objecting to this process in District Court, the employer is required to immediately start withholding money. It is paid to the Department of Human Services and the Department will send it on to you.

If you have questions about this process, call the Support Enforcement Division of your local Department of Human Services office.

A blank copy of the Conditional Order of Income Withholding is in the Appendix. A sample completed form is provided here as Form 7.

Instructions for Completing Conditional Order of Income Withholding

The letters below correspond to letters on the sample completed Form 7.

A through E will be the same information as on the Complaint and other forms.

F. Leave blank (the court will fill it in)

G. The full name of the spouse who will be paying child support

H. Leave blank (the court will fill it in)

I. Leave blank (the court will fill it in)

J. The full name of the spouse receiving child support

K. The full name of the spouse paying child support

L. Leave blank (the court will fill it in)

M. Leave blank (the court will fill it in)

FORM 7

STATE OF MAINE

Superior Court
______________________, ss.
Docket No. ______________

District Court
Division of Eastern Cumberland [A]
Location Brunswick, Maine [B]
Docket No. ______________ [C]

D] SUSAN T. BROWN

Plaintiff

vs.

E] JOHN D. BROWN

Defendant

CONDITIONAL ORDER OF INCOME WITHHOLDING (19 M.R.S.A. §777)

This Conditional Order of Income Withholding is incorporated in, and is a part of, the [Divorce Judgment] [Order] of this court dated ______________. [F]

It is ORDERED that the payor of income to John D. Brown [G]
(obligor)
from any source shall withhold from any amounts due the obligor, and shall pay to the Maine Department of Human Services, at least monthly, the sum of $ [H] per [I], which is the obligor's current support and/or alimony obligation, together with an additional sum to be applied toward any arrearage of support or alimony owed by the obligor, notice of which has been served on the payor with a copy of this withholding order. However, the total amount withheld by the payor shall not be greater than the maximum allowed by 19 M.R.S.A. §502 and 15 U.S.C. § 1673. So long as any arrearage remains outstanding, the amount of withholding by the payor shall be the maximum permitted by these statutes.

It is further ORDERED that Susan T. Brown [J] shall not serve
(obligee)
a copy of this withholding order on any payor of income until the provisions of 19 M.R.S.A. §777(1)(B)(1),(2),(4) and (5) have been met.

IMPORTANT NOTICE TO John D. Brown [K]:
Withholding of your income may result if you fail to make the support or alimony payments that the court has ordered you to make. However, no withholding shall take place until the following conditions are met:

(1) You request the withholding of your income, or

(2) Your child support or alimony payments are in arrears in an amount equal to one month's support or alimony and you are notified of that arrearage in writing.

(3) The obligee must give you written notice of the amount of the arrearages at least 20 days before serving a copy of this order on the payor of income. During the 20 day period you may dispute the amount of the arrearage by filing a motion in this court asking the court to determine the amount in arrears. At the same time you may ask the court for a stay (delay) of service of this order on the payor. The court may issue a stay of not more than 60 days.

It is further ORDERED that this order be noted upon the docket by incorporation by reference pursuant to Rule 79(a).

Dated: ______________ [L]

______________ [M]
Judge, District Court
Justice, Superior Court

DCCV-45 1-87
CV-51 1-87

i. PROPERTY LIST

By rule, both the husband and wife together or separately must file a list of personal and marital property **at least three days** before the scheduled hearing date. If you have not filed this list, some judges will refuse to hear your case on that date, even if you only have personal property. If your spouse is unavailable or unwilling to sign a property list, you should file your list anyway. Ask the judge to make an order based on your list. If the judge refuses, ask for the hearing to be continued and talk with a lawyer.

Some courts provide a form "Property List." The blank form in the Appendix would probably be accepted as a Property List in any District Court in Maine, but you should check with the Court Clerk to make sure that this style is acceptable in that Court. The blank form in the Appendix may be photocopied for use in your divorce if one is not available from the court. The following Form 8 is a completed sample Property List, using that form.

Remember that the point of this list is to tell the Court which items of property are in dispute and which are not. You do not have to list every single thing you own on the list. Instead, you should list the things which have some value and all specific things which are in dispute, no matter how little "market value" they might have.

FORM 8

RULE 80 (n) PROPERTY LIST

[Mark with an X all items in dispute]

REAL PROPERTY (land, land and buildings):

Located at: Back Road, Freeport, Maine

Described in deed of T. & M. Smith to Susan & John Brown

Registry of Deeds, Book 4449, Page 34.

This real property is (marital) ~~X(non-marital of ____________)XX~~

(If more than one deed, attach a list with similar information.)

PERSONAL PROPERTY (clothing, furniture, vehicles, recreational equipment, bank accounts, stock, and other personal property. General references often will be sufficient and each individual item usually need not be listed.)

Items of Property	Check if Marital	If non-marital, list owner
18' Wooden Canoe		Susan Brown
Antique Dining Room Table & Chairs		Susan Brown
All other property now in the possession of Susan Brown		Susan Brown
Cold-plated flute		John Brown
1976 Red Ford Mustang	X	
1978 Blue Saab Stationwagon	X	
Pioneer stereo system	X	
Color TV and VCR	X	
Antique gold pocket watch		John Brown
All other property now in the possession of John Brown		John Brown

Date *Oct 31, 1988*

Susan T. Brown
Signature

j. CHILD SUPPORT AFFIDAVITS AND WORKSHEET

In all divorces involving children, the courts must now award child support based on a table and a set of guidelines. This table is reprinted in Appendix II. (Check with the court to see if the table has been updated since this book was printed.)

In every case, the amount of child support ordered will be based on the information provided on the "Affidavit of Income and Assets" and the "Child Support Worksheet". Form 9 is the Affidavit of Income and Assets; Form 10 is the Child Support Worksheet. Pick up these forms from your court clerk. Samples of these forms are completed in this section. Blank copies of the forms are in Appendix III for you to look at or use as a draft. It may be helpful to look at these forms now, before you read the explanation for filling them out.

You and your spouse should each fill out your own "Affidavit of Income and Assets" described in this section. You should exchange these forms with each other before mediation and file both forms with the court three (3) days before the hearing. The "Child Support Worksheet" should be filled out using the information on your income affidavit and your spouse's income affidavit.

If your spouse will not fill out an affidavit, you should be prepared to answer the judge's questions about your spouse's income, employment history and other financial information. If you don't know this information and can't find it out, explain this to the judge at the hearing. Try filling out an Income Affidavit for your spouse using your best guess of his or her income and financial information.

If you have trouble with these forms, don't panic! These are hard forms to figure out. If you need help, you and your spouse could bring the forms *and all the information needed to fill them out* to mediation and then ask the mediator for help. You can also hire a lawyer just to help you with these forms. A relatively inexpensive place to get a lawyer's help is through the Maine Bar Association Lawyer Referral and Information Service where you could ask for a half-hour consultation to help you with the forms. The number for the Maine Bar Association Lawyer Referral Service is 622-1460.

"THE AFFIDAVIT OF INCOME AND ASSETS"
HEADING

A through E: Fill out the heading (caption) just as you have on all of the other forms that you have prepared for the court.

F. Your full married name.

G. Your mailing address.

H. Your Social Security number.

NOTE: If you have a particular reason for not wanting to fill in some of the questions listed above, leave them blank and explain your reason to the judge at the hearing.

GROSS INCOME (Page 1)

Section 1 - Wages, Salary, Self-Employment Income

1.1: List the total amount of gross income (before taxes, social security and other deductions are taken out) that you earned in the *last calendar year*. If you were self-employed, list your income after deducting your business expenses. (This is the amount that you listed for the IRS on Schedule C.) Attach a copy of Schedule C if you have one. Remember to attach a copy of your W-2 form from *last* year, a recent pay stub from *this* year, or other proof of earnings.

NOTE: Gross income can also include the difference between what someone is now earning and what that person is capable of earning. Therefore, when you look at your spouse's affidavit, if you feel that he or she could be earning more and therefore providing more support, then you may want to discuss this with your spouse. If you cannot reach agreement about this issue, you may make this claim to the court by telling the judge at the hearing that your spouse can earn more and why. If your spouse is caring for his or her children or other dependents in the home, be sure to mention this because it effects your spouse's ability to work outside the home.

1.2: List each person or business you have worked for *this calendar year.* If self-employed, put "self-employed".

1.3: List the period of time you worked for each person or business listed on the same line under 1.2.

1.4: List the total gross income you had from wages or self-employment so far this year from each employer listed on the same line under 1.2.

1.5: List the total gross annual income you expect to have from wages or self-employment *this calendar year.*

Section 2 - Other Income

2.1: List the source of any *unearned* income from the *last calendar year.* Unearned income means any other income you had that you did not list in Section 1, like alimony, social security, unemployment benefits, workers' compensation, disability benefits (but not SSI), retirement or pension income, rental or mortgage income, interest, capital gains or any other income.

NOTE: Income does **not** include AFDC (Aid to Families with Dependent Children), SSI (Supplemental Security Income), food stamps, or general assistance from your city or town.

2.2: List when you received the income from the source listed on line 2.1.

2.3: List the total amount of income you received from each source during the *last calendar year.*

2.4: List the amount of unearned income you expect you will have received *this calendar year.* (Remember, do **not** include, AFDC, SSI, food stamps or general assistance.) If you think that the unearned income that you received last calendar year is a good estimate of what you expect to receive this year, then list the total amount that you listed at 2.3 above. But if you do not think that last year's total unearned income is a good estimate of the unearned income you will be receiving this year, then put down the amount you expect to receive this calendar year here. Simply write down underneath the amount "estimate for this year" so that the court will know that it is for this year. (See Form 9 for example).

Section 3. - Fringe Benefits

3.1: List the annual value of benefits from employment that you expect to receive *this calendar year.* Only include benefits paid for by your employer that actually reduce your personal day-to-day living expenses. For example, if your employer gives you a house or car for *personal* (not work-related) use, list the annual rental value of the house or car.

List only the annual value of the health insurance premiums that *your employer pays for you.* Do not include the value of the premiums that are paid by your employer for the benefit of your children. How courts will consider the value of health insurance is still somewhat up in the air. If you do list health insurance as a fringe benefit, write "health insurance" next to the amount so that the court will know what the amount is for.

Section 4 - Total Annual Gross Income

4.1: Add together the dollar amounts in 1.5, 2.4 and 3.1 of the form and list the answer here. This is your total annual gross income for this calendar year.

PROPERTY AND ASSETS (Page 2)

NOTE: You should list the same property here that is on your property list (see Section i and Form 8 in this chapter); except do not list non-marital property belonging to your spouse.

Section 5 - Vehicles

In this section, "vehicle" means not only cars and trucks, but snowmobiles, motorcycles, all terrain vehicles, boats, campers, etc.

5.1: List the type and year of vehicle(s).

5.2: List the value of the vehicle. This is the amount you think you could get if you sold it on the open market. (Ask a dealer to estimate the value for you.)

5.3: List the amount you still owe on the vehicle. Do not include the interest you are paying on the loan in the amount you owe. (Ask the place you borrowed the money from to give you this information if you do not know.)

5.4: Subtract the amount you owe on the vehicle (5.3) from its value (5.2), and list the answer here.

Section 6 - Personal Property

Only list items of personal property (such as gems, antiques, artwork, etc.) worth over $3,000 in this section.

6.1: List what the item is.

6.2: List the value of the item. This is the amount you think you could get if you sold it. (You may want to ask a dealer of such items to estimate the value for you.)

6.3: List the amount you still owe on the item. (Ask the place you borrowed the money from to give you this information.)

6.4: Subtract the amount you owe on the item (6.3) from its value (6.2) and list your answer here.

Section 7 - Real Estate

7.1: A simple description of the property is enough. (See example at Form 9.)

7.2: To find out the value of the property, ask a real estate broker what it could be sold for. (You do not need to pay for a formal appraisal, a broker's estimate is good enough.)

7.3: The bank or other lender that you make your payments to "holds" the mortgage. Ask the lender how much you still owe on it. Do not include interest payments that you will be paying in the future.

7.4: Subtract the mortgage amount (7.3) from the value (7.2) and list the result here. This is your "net value" or "equity" in the property.

Section 8 - Bank Accounts

This section is self-explanatory.

Section 9 - Other Property

This section is for any other property that you have not already listed. For example, if you are expecting a large lump sum payment of worker's compensation or Social Security or some other benefit, it would be listed here. Don't list it unless you are quite sure you will be receiving it. (Remember, however, SSI, AFDC, food stamps and general assistance from your city or town should not be included.)

EXPENSES RELATING TO CHILD SUPPORT WORKSHEET (Page 3)

Section 11 - Child Support

This section involves child support for children from a different relationship *who are not in your home now and whc are not involved in this divorce.* You should list child support you are paying for these children, voluntarily, under a court order, or under an order of the Department of Human Services. You should also list any *alimony* to a former spouse you are paying under an earlier court order. If you have listed alimony, simply put "(alimony)" next to the weekly amount on the form.

The form asks who you pay the money to. If you pay your support to the Department of Human Services, say so.

The form asks for a *weekly* amount. If you pay monthly, divide the monthly amount by 4.33 (the average number of weeks in a month) and list your answer.

Section 12 - Other Children

List your natural or adopted children *who are living in your home now, but are not involved in this divorce.* This would include children at home from a prior marriage, for example.

Section 13 - Medical Insurance

This section asks you to list medical insurance you pay for yourself separate from that which you pay for your children.

You will probably have to ask your medical insurer or your employer to separate out the cost of insuring you from the cost of insuring your children so that you can list them separately on the form. This section only includes costs that you have. If your employer pays everything, then list "0". If you have no health insurance, then list "uninsured".

13.1: List the yearly cost you pay for your health insurance.

13.2: List the yearly cost you pay for your children's health insurance.

13.3: Add the amounts in 13.1 and 13.2 and list your total yearly cost for health insurance.

Section 14 - Child Care Costs

List your weekly child care costs for work, school or job training.

Section 15 - Extraordinary Medical Expenses

"Extraordinary medical expenses" means those recurring annual medical expenses for the children that are over $150. It is normal to pay about $150 per year for medical expenses for colds, flu and checkups. Any expenses that you expect will continue and that are over and above $150 are "extraordinary" and should be listed here. The form asks for a weekly amount, so divide your best estimate of your annual medical expenses over $150 by 52 weeks.

Section 16 - Other Expenses

This section is for unusual expenses or large debts that you think the court should consider as a reason to set a child support order that is different than the one you will work out on the child support worksheet. You should fill out the worksheet that follows, find out how the child support award comes out, and decide if you want a different amount, before you fill this section out.

NOTE: Be sure to sign this form before a Notary Public or Clerk of Court. Do not forget to attach your most recent W-2 form and a recent pay stub from this year or other proof of earnings.

FORM 9

STATE OF MAINE

SUPERIOR COURT

_____________________, ss.

CV-_____________________

DISTRICT COURT
Division of Eastern Cumberland [A]
Location Brunswick, Maine [B]
Docket No. _____________________ [C]

[D] Susan T. Brown *Plaintiff*

vs.

AFFIDAVIT of INCOME and ASSETS

[E] John D. Brown *Defendant*

Name Susan T. Brown [F] Social Security No. 000-00-0000 [H]
Address Back Road Freeport Maine 04032 [G]
Street *Town* *State* *Zip*

GROSS INCOME

1. WAGES, SALARY, SELF-EMPLOYMENT INCOME

(Attach a copy of your most recent W-2 Form and your most recent pay stub.)

How much did you earn in the last calendar year? $ 12,000 [1.1]

How much have you earned so far this year?

Employer	Dates	Amount	
self-employed [1.2]	1/90 - 3/90 [1.3]	2,500	[1.4]
Carpenter's Inc.	4/90 - Present	5,000	

Estimated total of wages, salary, self-employment income this year $ 9,000 [1.5]

2. OTHER INCOME

List any other income received last year from any source such as alimony, social security, unemployment benefits, workers' compensation, disability, pension income, insurance, rental or mortgage income, bonuses, interest, dividends, capital gains or money from any other source except AFDC, SSI, general assistance or food stamps:

Source	Dates	Amount	
Unemployment benefits [2.1]	10/89 - 12/89 [2.2]	1,200	[2.3]
Maine Bank interest	1/89 - 12/89	28	

Total $ 1,000 [2.4]
Estimate for this year

3. FRINGE BENEFITS

List value of benefits received through employment which reduce your living expenses such as a car, housing, insurance or meals $ 0 [3.1]

4. TOTAL ANNUAL GROSS INCOME $ 10,000 [4.1]
(Add the amounts from 1, 2 and 3 above)

DCCV-51 (7/90)

PROPERTY AND ASSETS

5. VEHICLES

List any motor vehicles, including motorcycles, snowmobiles, boats, etc. Attach a separate sheet if needed.

Item	Value	Amount owed on item	Net value
1986 Mustang **[5.1]**	3,500 **[5.2]**	1,500 **[5.3]**	2,000 **[5.4]**
1988 V.W.	8,000	6,500	1,500
Canoe	700	0	700

6. PERSONAL PROPERTY

List any item of personal property worth more that $3000 such as gems, works of art, furniture, antiques, collections, or other items of investment vaule. Attach a separate sheet if needed.

Item	Value	Amount owed on item	Net value
Antique Dining Set **[6.1]**	3,500 **[6.2]**	0 **[6.3]**	3,500 **[6.4]**

7. REAL ESTATE

List all real estate that you own, including your home. Attach a separate sheet if needed.

Description and location	Value	Mortgage	Net value
Home and 1 acre in Freeport **[7.1]**	90,000 **[7.2]**	75,000 **[7.3]**	15,000 **[7.4]**

8. BANK ACCOUNTS

List all accounts you have in financial institutions, such as banks, credit unions. Include savings and checking accounts, certificates of deposit, etc. Attach a separate sheet if needed.

Name of financial institution	Type of account	Amount
Maine Bank	checking	525.00 **[8]**

9. OTHER PROPERTY

List separately other property such as stocks, bonds, notes, trusts, annuities, pensions, deferred compensation, IRAs, or money that people owe you. Attach a separate sheet if needed.

Property	Value
Expecting worker's compensation settlement	1,500 **[9]**

EXPENSES RELATING TO CHILD SUPPORT WORKSHEET

11. CHILD SUPPORT

List child support you pay for children who are not a subject of this action

Name of child	To whom paid	Weekly amount	
None			[11]

12. OTHER CHILDREN

List other children living in your home who are not the subject of this action and whom you are legally obligated to support.

Name of child	Date of birth	Relationship to you	Name of child	Date of birth	Relationship to you	
None						[12]

13. MEDICAL INSURANCE

Cost of medical insurance you pay for yourself per year 1,500 [13.1]

Additional cost of medical insurance you pay for your children per year 2,000 [13.2]

Total 3,500 [13.3]

14. CHILD CARE COSTS

Amount of weekly child care costs you pay so you can work (or train to work) 65 [14]

15. EXTRAORDINARY MEDICAL EXPENSES

Name of child	Reason for expense	Weekly amount	
Sally J. Brown	Diabetes	20.00	[15]

16. OTHER EXPENSES

List any other large debts you owe or other exceptionally high expenses for you or your children that you feel justify a deviation from the Child Support Guidelines.

None [16]

☒ I have attached a copy of my most recent W-2 form. ☒ I have attached a copy of my most recent pay stub.

The above financial statement is complete and includes all assets and income I receive and is based on my own personal knowledge, information and belief, and to the extent it is based on information and belief, I believe such information to be true.

Dated: October 22, 1990

Susan T. Brown
Signature

Personally appeared the above named Susan T. Brown and made oath to the foregoing affidavit, before me:

Dated: October 22, 1990

Jane S. Jones
(~~Attorney~~) (Notary Public) (~~Deputy Clerk~~)

A COPY OF THIS AFFIDAVIT AND THE CHILD SUPPORT WORKSHEET MUST BE PROVIDED TO THE OTHER PARTY BEFORE MEDIATION. THIS AFFIDAVIT AND THE CHILD SUPPORT WORKSHEET MUST BE FILED WITH THE COURT CLERK 3 DAYS BEFORE THE COURT HEARING.

"CHILD SUPPORT WORKSHEET"

This form helps you and the court decide what amount should be paid in child support. It will be based on the information you and your spouse have listed on each of your "Affidavits of Income and Assets". Be sure to fill in this form with information from the affidavits of *both* you and your spouse. If your spouse won't fill out his or her own Affidavit, then put your best guess of his or her income and assets on an affidavit form. File it with your own Affidavit and explain to the judge at the hearing why you filled it out yourself.

The form refers to the **"primary care provider"** and the **"non-primary care provider"**. The parent who will have the children more than 70% of the time is the primary care provider. The parent who has the children less than 30% of the time is the non-primary care provider. If you and your spouse intend to split your time with the children more evenly than that, tell the court. The court may decide that the amount of support that is figured by doing the worksheet is not right. (See the list of reasons for deviating from the child support table in Appendix II.) You should do the worksheet anyway; list the parent that you expect will have the children most often as the primary care provider and list the other parent as the non-primary care provider. Write in your name and your spouse's name at the top of the columns.

A through D: The heading should be filled in just like all the other forms that you have filled out for the court.

E. List all the children that you and your spouse have. Do not include children over 17 unless they are 18 and still full time students in secondary school (high school or vocational school). Do not include your children from other relationships.

Line 1 - Annual Gross Income

List the amounts stated on line 4 of the Affidavits of Income and Assets of both you and your spouse. Check to be sure each parent's income is in the correct column. Remember if one parent's income is AFDC or SSI that parent's annual gross income will be listed as "zero".

Line 1(a) - Pre-existing Support

List child support for children from a different relationship that is currently being paid. Refer to paragraph 11 of the Affidavits of Income and Assets of you and your spouse. Because you need an *annual* amount on the worksheet, multiply the total of the weekly amounts listed in paragraph 11 by 52 weeks and list the answer.

Line 1(b) - Health Insurance Premium

List the amount that each parent pays for the children that is listed in paragraph 13 of both parents' Affidavits of Income and Assets.

Line 1(c) - Responsibility for Other Children of Non-Primary Care Provider

You do not have to fill in this line unless the non-primary care provider has children from another relationship living with him or her. (See paragraph 12 of the Affidavit of Income and Assets.)

If the non-primary care provider *does* have children from another relationship living with him/her, then the worksheet allows him or her to deduct the cost of caring for those children. This cost is calculated by using the child support table. Figure that cost for line 1(c) as follows:

Step 1: On a scrap piece of paper, write the total amount of the non-primary care provider's gross income listed on line 1 above.

Step 2: Then subtract any amounts under the non-primary care provider's name listed on lines 1(a) and 1(b) above.

Step 3: Look at the Child Support Table ("Schedule of Basic Weekly Child Support Entitlements") in Appendix II of this book. This table will give you weekly child support amounts for *each* child.

You will use either the left side of the chart for each child age 0-11 or the right side for each child age 12-17. Find the amount of gross income on the table that is closest to your answer to Step 2. Draw a line across the page from that number. Now, at the top of the page, find the number that is the same as the number of children that are in the non-primary care provider's home. (Include only natural or adopted children and don't include children involved in this divorce.)

Look down this column. When you reach the place where this column and the line you drew across the page meet, you will find the number that is the basic weekly support entitlement for that child.

Step 4: Repeat this process for each child and add together these amounts. Then add any child care costs or extraordinary medical expenses that the non-primary care provider has for his or her children in the household. Write in this total at line 1(c).

> **For example:** A married couple with children is getting divorced. The man has been living apart from his wife for a year and has a 9 month old baby from a new relationship that is living with him. He earns $22,000 a year. He has no child care costs or extraordinary medical expenses. His cost of caring for the baby now living with him is figured by looking at the child support table in Appendix II. He would first look across the page at the income level shown on the table of $22,200. (This is the number closest to his actual income of $22,000.) He would then look down the "one-child" column for children under 12, to get the child support amount of $62 per week. His cost for this one child is $62 x 52 = $3,224.00 a year. He would write $3,224.00 at Line 1(c) for the non-primary care provider on the Child Support Worksheet.

Now here is the tricky part:

> **Further Example:** Suppose in addition to his baby, the man in the above example has a teenage son living with him from an earlier relationship. For the baby's support, look, once again, across from the gross income of $22,200. But this time, look down the column for *two* children in the ages 0-11 category and find the amount of support. It is $48.
>
> For the teenager, do the same thing again, this time using the column for *two* children in the ages 12-17 category. The support is $59.
>
> Now add $48 and $59 to get $107. This is a *weekly* support amount, so multiply it by 52. The annual support will be $5,564. The man would put $5,564 in Line 1(c).

Line 3 - Proportional Share of Gross Income

"Proportional share of gross income" means the percent of combined income from line 2 that is yours and the percent that is your spouse's. For example, assume the combined income on line 2 is $23,000. If your portion is $8,000 and your spouse's is $15,000, your proportional share is 35%. ($8,000 divided by $23,000 = .35). Your spouse's proportional share is 65% ($15,000 divided by $23,000 = .65). Remember that the two percentage amounts should add up to 100%. (See example on Form 10). If one parent has only had AFDC or SSI income for the whole calendar year, the other parent has 100% of the child support obligation.

Line 4 - Basic Weekly Support Entitlement From Table

Before you can fill out the section of the child support worksheet under line 4, you must learn to use the Child Support Table in Appendix II.

You will find weekly child support amounts by a three step process. You will have to do this for each child involved in the divorce.

Step 1: Look at the Table and the example at Form 11. Notice that it is divided into two parts. The left side is for children ages 0-11. The right is for children ages 12-17. (If your child is 18 and still a student, you should use the right side of the table.)

Step 2: For each child, look on the side of the table that fits the age of that child. Then look under the "parents' combined annual gross income" column for the number that is closest to your and your spouse's *combined* income given on Line 2 of the child support worksheet. From that number, draw a line across the page.

Step 3: Find the column underneath the *total* number of children involved in the divorce. For example, if you have two children under 12 and one over 12, you would use the column for three children even though you have fewer than that in each age category. (See example on Form 11.)

Step 4: Look down this column. When you reach the place where this column and the line you drew across the page meet, you will find the number that is the basic weekly support entitlement for that child. (See example on Form 11.)

Step 5: Repeat the above steps to find the basic weekly support entitlement for each additional child. Be sure to use the correct side of the table, depending on the age of each child.

Now you are ready to begin filling in the blanks in the section under Line 4 of the Child Support Worksheet.

CHILDREN AGES 0-11

4(a): Write in the total number of children involved in your divorce in both age categories.

4(b): Write in the amount from the table of the basic weekly support entitlement for one of your children under 12. (See Step 4 above.)

NOTE: A space labeled "b" also appears on the next line down. Write the same number in here.

4(c): Write in the number of children involved in the divorce who are under 12.

4(d): Multiply the number of your children under 12 by the basic weekly support obligation for each of those children. Write the answer here. (In other words, the number in 4(c) x 4(b) = 4(d).)

CHILDREN AGES 12-17

4(a): Write in the total number of children involved in your divorce. This should be the same number as you wrote in 4(a) for the 0-11 age category.

4(e): Write in the amount from the table of the basic weekly support entitlement for one of your children over 12.

NOTE: A space labeled "e" also appears on the next line down. Write in the same number in here.

4(f): Write in the number of the children involved in your divorce that are 12 and over.

4(g): Multiply the number of your children that are 12 and over by the basic weekly support obligation for each of those children. Write the answer here. (In other words, the number in 4(f) x 4(e) = 4(g).)

4(h): Add the amount in 4(d) to the amount in 4(g) and write your answer here.

Line 5 - Weekly Child Care and Extraordinary Medical Expenses

Child Care Costs: List each child involved in the divorce for whom child care is paid and the weekly amount of that care. In **(i)** write in the total weekly child care costs. This should be the same as the amount on Line 14 of the primary care provider's Affidavit of Income and Assets.

Recurring Extraordinary Medical Expenses: List the information provided in Line 15 of the primary care provider's Affidavit of Income and Assets and put the weekly amount on Line (j).

Total Weekly Support Obligation - Line (k)

Add the amounts from **(h)**, **(i)** and **(j)** and put your answer at Line **(k)**.

Line 6 - Weekly Parental Support

Multiply the amount from Line (k) by the primary care provider's "proportional share of gross income" on Line 3 of the worksheet. Put your answer under the space labeled "primary care provider spends directly".

Now, multiply the amount from (k) by the non-primary care provider's "proportional share of gross income" on Line 3 of the worksheet and put this answer under "non-primary care provider pays as support".

The amount in the block labeled "non-primary care provider pays as support" is the amount of weekly child support the court will award in your divorce.

If this has been hard to follow, the following example may help.

> **EXAMPLE:** Look at the sample child support worksheet and table that follows (Forms 10 and 11). They are filled out for the family in the following example.
>
> In this example, the mother has custody of three children: two under 12 and one who is 13. Her total gross income for this year is $10,000. She pays $65 per week in child care for the two children under 12. One child has diabetes, which costs $20 per week in medication that is not covered by insurance. Also, Mom has to pay for health insurance which costs $2,000 per year for the children plus another $1,000 for herself.
>
> The father's total gross income for this year is $18,000. He pays $3,000 per year in child support for children from an earlier marriage.

On Forms 10 and 11, you can see how this family uses the combined adjusted gross income of $23,000 from Line 3 of the worksheet (Form 10). The table (Form 11) shows a weekly support amount of $41 for each of the two children under 12 and $50 for the child over 12. Then the worksheet adds in the child care and medical expenses to find a total weekly support amount. The support amount is then divided between the parents in proportion to their income. It is assumed that the Mom provides her share simply because she cares for the children most of the time. Dad, however, must pay his share ($141.05) to Mom.

FORM 10

STATE OF MAINE

SUPERIOR COURT

______________________, ss.

CV-______________________

DISTRICT COURT

Division of Eastern Cumberland [A]

Docket No. ______________ [B]

[C] Susan T. Brown *Plaintiff*

vs.

[D] John D. Brown *Defendant*

CHILD SUPPORT WORKSHEET

Children	Date of Birth	Children	Date of Birth
[E] Sally J. Brown	1/22/90		
Nathan J. Brown	5/20/88		
Mary P. Brown	9/30/78		

	Primary Care Provider Name: Susan Brown	Non-Primary Care Provider Name: John Brown	Combined
1. Annual Gross Income	$ 10,000	$18,000	
a. Minus preexisting support 19 M.R.S.A. §311(5)(E)	0	3,000	
b. Minus health insurance premium §311(5)(F)	2,000	0	
c. Minus responsibility for other children of non-primary care provider §316(4)(A)	0	0	
2. Annual Gross Income (Adjusted)	$ 8,000	$15,000	$23,000
3. Proportional Share of Gross Income (each parent's income divided by combined income)	35 %	65 %	

4. Basic Weekly Support Entitlement from Table:

Children 0 --11 Category:

(a) Total No. Children 3 at Combined Gross Income (Adjusted) per table (b) $ 41

(c) Number of children 0--11 2 x amount at (b) $ 41 = (d) $ 82.00

Children 12 --17 Category:

(a) Total No. Children 3 at Combined Gross Income (Adjusted) per table (e) $ 50

(f) Number of children 12--17 1 x amount at (e) $ 50 = (g) $ 50.00

Basic Weekly Support Entitlement: *(Sum of (d) and (g))* = (h) $ 132.00

5. Weekly Child Care and Extraordinary Medical Expenses

Child Care Costs: (19 M.R.S.A. § 316(2)(A)

Name and amount per child per week: Sally J. Brown $ 32.50

Nathan J. Brown $ 32.50

$ ______

$ ______ = (i) $ 65.00

Recurring Extraordinary Medical Expenses: (19 M.R.S.A. § 316(2)(B)

Name and amount per child per week: Sally J. Brown $ 20.00 = (j) $ 20.00

TOTAL WEEKLY SUPPORT OBLIGATION: *(Sum of (h), (i) and (j)* = (k) $ 217.00

6. Weekly Parental Support Obligation *Line 3 times (k)*	Primary care provider spends directly	Non-primary care provider pays as support
	$ 75.95	$ 141.05

Submitted By: Susan T. Brown

~~(Attorney for)~~ (Plantiff) ~~(Defendant)~~

DCCV-50 (7/90)

SCHEDULE OF BASIC WEEKLY CHILD SUPPORT ENTITLEMENTS
(PER CHILD, PER WEEK, ROUNDED TO THE NEAREST DOLLAR)

Parents' Combined Annual Gross Income	Ages of Children: Age 0 thru 11 Years — Number of Children: 1	2	3	4	5	6	Parents' Combined Annual Gross Income	Ages of Children: Age 12 thru 17 Years — Number of Children: 1	2	3	4	5	6
$6,000	16	9	6	4	4	3	$6,000	17	9	6	5	4	3
$6,600	22	12	8	6	5	4	$6,600	23	12	8	6	5	4
$7,200	26	15	10	8	7	5	$7,200	30	16	11	8	7	6
$7,800	28	18	13	10	8	7	$7,800	35	19	13	10	8	7
$8,400	30	21	15	12	9	8	$8,400	37	23	15	12	9	8
$9,000	32	24	17	13	11	9	$9,000	39	26	18	13	11	9
$9,600	33	26	20	15	12	10	$9,600	41	30	20	15	12	10
$10,200	35	27	22	17	14	11	$10,200	43	33	22	17	14	11
$10,800	36	28	24	18	15	12	$10,800	45	35	24	19	15	13
$11,400	38	30	25	20	16	14	$11,400	47	37	27	20	16	14
$12,000	40	31	26	22	17	15	$12,000	49	38	29	22	18	15
$12,600	41	32	27	22	19	16	$12,600	51	39	31	23	19	16
$13,200	43	33	28	23	20	17	$13,200	53	41	33	25	20	17
$13,800	44	34	29	24	21	18	$13,800	54	42	35	27	22	18
$14,400	46	35	30	25	22	19	$14,400	56	44	37	28	23	19
$15,000	47	37	31	26	23	20	$15,000	58	45	38	30	24	20
$15,600	48	38	31	27	23	21	$15,600	60	47	39	32	25	21
$16,200	50	39	32	27	24	21	$16,200	61	48	40	33	27	22
$16,800	51	40	33	28	24	22	$16,800	63	49	41	35	28	23
$17,400	52	40	34	29	25	22	$17,400	64	50	42	35	29	24
$18,000	53	41	35	29	25	23	$18,000	66	51	43	36	30	25
$18,600	54	42	35	30	26	23	$18,600	67	52	44	37	31	26
$19,200	56	43	36	31	27	24	$19,200	69	53	45	38	33	27
$19,800	57	44	37	31	27	24	$19,800	70	55	46	39	34	28
$20,400	58	45	38	32	28	25	$20,400	72	56	46	39	34	29
$21,000	59	46	38	32	28	25	$21,000	73	57	47	40	35	30
$21,600	60	47	39	33	29	26	$21,600	75	58	48	41	36	31
$22,200	62	48	40	34	29	26	$22,200	76	59	49	42	36	32
$22,800	63	49	41	34	30	27	$22,800	78	60	50	43	37	33
$23,400	64	50	41	35	31	27	$23,400	79	61	51	43	38	34
$24,000	65	51	42	36	31	28	$24,000	80	63	52	44	39	34
$24,600	66	51	43	36	32	28	$24,600	82	64	53	45	39	35
$25,200	67	52	44	37	32	29	$25,200	83	65	54	46	40	35
$25,800	69	53	44	38	33	29	$25,800	85	66	55	46	40	36
$26,400	70	54	45	38	33	30	$26,400	86	67	56	47	41	37
$27,000	71	55	46	39	34	30	$27,000	87	68	57	48	42	37
$27,600	72	56	47	39	34	31	$27,600	89	69	58	49	42	38
$28,200	73	57	47	40	35	31	$28,200	90	70	58	49	43	38
$28,800	74	58	48	41	36	32	$28,800	92	71	59	50	44	39
$29,400	76	58	49	41	36	32	$29,400	93	72	60	51	45	40
$30,000	77	59	50	42	37	33	$30,000	95	74	61	52	45	40

Does the amount of support you figured on the table seem too high or too low for your family?

If the amount of support from the worksheet is not what you want for your family, a court may order a different amount. However, the court will do this only if you ask it to, and only if you give a specific reason why it should. A list of reasons that the court will consider is listed in the "Criteria For Deviating From Support Guidelines" found in Appendix II of this book.

If you want the court to order a different amount of child support than the amount on your worksheet, then tell the judge how much you want at the hearing and be ready to explain why your situation fits one of the reasons listed in Appendix II.

CONFUSED? If so, remember that you can hire an attorney just for the purpose of helping you with the child support forms. The more you prepare before meeting with the attorney, the cheaper it will be. You can also get half an hour of legal advice for a reasonable fee by contacting the Maine Bar Association's Lawyer Referral and Information Service (622-1460).

Chapter 11

Serve Your Spouse

INTRODUCTION

After you have purchased and filled out your Complaint and Summons (and Child Custody Affidavit if you and your spouse have children), these papers must be "served" on your spouse to notify him or her that you are beginning a divorce action.

You will have your spouse served with the court papers in one of five ways, depending on your circumstances.

In most cases, your spouse will be living in Maine and you will know where he or she is living. In this case, you will have the papers served personally on your spouse by a sheriff. You will only have to read **Section a, Service by Sheriff.**

If your spouse is living in another state, and you know his or her address, then you can have the papers "served" on your spouse by registered or certified mail. This is discussed in **Section b, Service by Registered or Certified Mail. But,** you may want to have your spouse served personally by a sheriff if:

(a) you are afraid your spouse will not sign for a certified letter, or

(b) you need service by a sheriff in order for the court to make an enforceable order for support or custody (See Chapter 6, Custody and Support: Jurisdiction).

If you don't know where your spouse is living, you will have to serve by publication. You should read **Section c, Service by Publication.**

If your spouse is in the military service, you must have him or her served according to special procedures. You should read **Section d, Service on Spouse in the Military.**

Finally, if your spouse is living outside the United States, then you must follow a different set of special procedures. These are described in **Section e, Service on a Spouse in a Foreign Country.**

If you have problems understanding these procedures, please talk with a lawyer. You can hire a lawyer just for the purpose of giving you advice or helping you make service on your spouse.

a. **SERVICE BY SHERIFF** (also called "personal" or "in-hand service")

Once you have prepared your papers, they will be ready for service on your spouse. You will have the following papers ready to give the sheriff:

1. One copy of the Divorce Complaint,
2. The original and one copy of the Divorce Summons, and
3. A copy of the Child Custody Affidavit (if one is necessary)

To arrange for personal service, first call the sheriff's office in the county where your spouse is living, working, or can be easily located. If your spouse is out of state **and** you want to make personal service, ask your local county sheriff to give you the address of the appropriate sheriff's department in that state.

Once you have learned the name and address of the deputy who serves the town where your spouse lives, either see him or her personally or write a letter explaining what you want done (see suggested deputy's letter at Form 12 at the end of this chapter). Be sure to tell the deputy where and when your spouse might most easily be served.

It is also perfectly legal for you to arrange for your spouse to pick up the papers at the deputy's office if your spouse is willing to do so. (This is cheaper since you will avoid the deputy's mileage charge).

The deputy will hand your spouse the papers which you have given him or her. The deputy will write on the original of the Summons to indicate that service has been made and return the original Summons to you.

While there is no standard fee, service costs in Maine average $15 at this time. There will also be an additional fee for mileage if the sheriff must travel a lot to make service, and postage if the papers must be mailed back to you. These additional charges will appear on Side 2 of your returned Summons. You should pay this bill promptly so that other people filing **pro se** will have no problem getting the sheriff to serve their papers because he or she hasn't been paid by others. It is possible that the sheriff may request payment "up front" before making service on your spouse. He or she may ask you for part of the payment before making service, and the rest after the papers have been served.

If you have filed an "Application to Proceed In Forma Pauperis" and it is granted by the Court, you can forward the deputy's bill directly to District Court for payment. In this case, you should get an "attested" copy of the judge's order permitting you to proceed without cost and give this to the sheriff when you deliver the papers for service so he or she will know from whom to expect payment.

b. SERVICE BY REGISTERED OR CERTIFIED MAIL (for out-of-state spouses)

Registered or Certified mail is commonly used to serve an out-of-state spouse unless there is a particular reason to do otherwise as discussed earlier in this chapter.

If you choose to serve by certified mail, you must send one copy of the Complaint, one copy of the Summons, and a Child Custody Affidavit (if one is necessary) to your spouse. You will have to go to the Post Office to do this. **Be sure to tell the postal clerk that you want to send the letter by "Certified Mail, Restricted Delivery, Return Receipt Requested."**

If your spouse accepts the certified letter, you will receive a green return receipt card in the mail. When you get this you must prepare an "Affidavit of Service," a paper in which you swear that you have made service on your spouse by certified mail. There is no court form for this legal paper; you must prepare it yourself. (See Form 13 below). An Affidavit of Service must be signed by you in the presence of a notary public.

If you have sent the letter to your spouse's current address but he/she refuses to accept the certified or registered letter, the post office will return the letter to you indicating on the envelope that it was "refused" (Be sure to save this envelope. You will have to attach it to your Affidavit). In this case, mail the papers again by regular mail. Your Affidavit of Service should say that your spouse refused to sign for the certified or registered letter and that you have mailed the papers to that address again by regular mail. (See Form 14 below).

c. SERVICE BY PUBLICATION

If you have made every reasonable effort to find your spouse but have been unsuccessful, service must be made by publishing notice that you are beginning a divorce action in a local newspaper. It does not matter whether your spouse actually sees the notice in the newspaper. The fact that you have published notice will satisfy the court that you have done all you can to tell your spouse that a divorce action has begun.

Service by publication is made as follows:

STEP 1 - Prepare your Divorce Complaint and Child Custody Affidavit (if one is necessary) as usual. Wherever the papers call for your spouse's address, use the words: "The residence of the Defendant is not known by the Plaintiff and cannot be ascertained by reasonable diligence." Be sure to complete the oath on the back of the Divorce Complaint (Form 1) and have it witnessed by a Notary Public.

STEP 2 - You must next get the court's permission to make service by Publication. In order to do this you must prepare the following papers:

A. A Motion for Service by Publication (Form 15)

B. An Affidavit describing all efforts that you have made to locate your spouse, that is signed by you in the presence of a Notary Public. (Form 16)

C. An order for the judge to sign, giving you permission to serve by Publication, (Form 17)

D. An original Petition and Order for Military Search and five copies for the judge to sign, authorizing a search to be made to determine if your spouse is in the military service. (Form 18)

Although only Form 18 can be purchased from the court, you should have no difficulty preparing the rest yourself if you model yours after the examples that follow. Only your "Affidavit in Support of Motion for Publication" may need to be changed somewhat from the example at Form 16 to reflect your individual situation. In preparing your Affidavit, be sure to describe **every** effort you have made to find your lost spouse.

When preparing your Motion, you must type in the name of the paper in which publication will be made. Although any daily or weekly paper of general circulation **in the county where the Complaint will be filed** will probably be acceptable, some are less expensive than others. You may want to compare prices before deciding on a particular paper. You may also want to check with the clerk in advance to be sure your choice will be approved. You should also check with the newspaper to learn the dates that legal notices are published and the deadlines for submitting legal notices for publication, in case the judge requests that information from you.

STEP 3 - Once you have prepared these forms, take them with your Complaint and Child Custody Affidavit (if one is necessary) to your court clerk. Request that your Orders be signed by a judge and "attested" by the clerk. You will probably not have to see a judge, but you might. If you do, he or she will probably only want to discuss the efforts you have made to find your spouse, or when the newspaper you have selected publishes legal advertisements. (**NOTE:** You do not have to prepare a "Summons" in cases of service by publication. The judge's order for service by publication and the publication itself will act as the Summons).

The judge will write in the date by which publication must begin on your Order for Publication.

STEP 4 - Send a copy of the signed Order for Service by Publication (Form 17 with a cover letter (Form 19) to the newspaper which you have selected. Enclose a verification form (Form 20) for the newspaper to fill out and return to you.

Publication must begin within 20 days of the day on which the judge signs your order. Be sure to make arrangements with the newspaper **immediately** to make sure that this deadline is met.

STEP 5 - Send one copy of your Order authorizing a military search, signed by the judge, with a cover letter (Form 21) to **each** branch of the military service at the addresses listed below. Include a check or money order for $5.20 and **a self-addressed stamped envelope in each letter.** Note to whom the check or money order should be made payable and whether any special notes go on the envelope.

Petition for Military Search Addresses:

1. Commandant (GPE-3/45)
   U.S. Coast Guard
   2100 Second Street, S.W.
   Washington, D.C. 20593

Mail with notation on envelope: DO NOT OPEN IN MAIL ROOM

Payable: United States Coast Guard
Amount: $5.20

2. Bonnie J. Jarrett
   Chief, Data Verification/Locater Section
   Department of the Army
   U.S. Army Enlisted Records and Evaluation Center
   Fort Benjamin
   Harrison, IN 46249-5301

Payable: Treasurer of the United States
Amount: $5.20

3. Commandant of the U.S. Marine Corps
   (Code MSRB-10)
   Headquarters, U.S. Marine Corps
   ATTENTION: R.R. Danatto
   Head Unit 3, Records Service
   Records Branch, Personnel Management Division
   Washington, D.C. 20380

Payable: Treasurer of the United States
Amount: $5.20

4. Chief of Navy Personnel
   PERS-17/NMPC-03
   ATTENTION: D.M. Dorsey
   Navy Department
   Naval Military Personnel Command
   Washington, D.C. 20370-5000

Payable: Treasurer of the United States
Amount: $5.20

5. Director of Personnel Data Systems
   HQ AFMPC/DPM0003
   9504 IH 35 North
   San Antonio, TX 78233-6636

Payable: Treasurer of the United States
Amount: $5.20

These addresses and costs change from time to time. If your letter is returned, ask your United States Senator or Representative's local office for the correct address.

STEP 6 - You will receive verification in the mail from:

A. The newspaper, indicating that notice has been published for three consecutive weeks, including copies of the notice as it appeared in the paper and the completed form which you sent to them; and

B. Each branch of the military service, indicating whether or not your spouse is enlisted. It often takes several months for verification to be returned from the various branches of the military service. If it takes a particularly long time to receive verification from one branch of the service, you might speed things up by either phoning the office to which you wrote, or asking your U.S. Representative or Senator to investigate the delay. (If you discover that your spouse is in the military service, you should read **Section d** of this chapter and must begin again following those instructions).

Service by publication is considered complete 21 days after the first notice appears in the newspaper. As in any other divorce case, you must wait for 60 days after this date before setting your court date. **But,** before you go to the hearing, you **must** have received each of the pieces of verification described above **and** filed them with the court clerk. If they haven't all arrived by that date, you should reschedule the hearing.

STEP 7 - You may now follow the remaining instructions in this manual without any further changes. Be sure to file a Federal Affidavit on the day of the hearing if you have learned that your spouse is not in the military service.

d. Service on a Spouse in the Military Service

If your spouse is in the active military service (not the Reserves) you must get his or her permission to be sued in a divorce action. Without permission, you will have to wait until he or she becomes a civilian again. This is a right that all military personnel have under the "Soldiers and Sailors Civil Relief Act."

If you are having difficulty getting your spouse to sign a waiver giving permission to be sued, and you don't want to wait until he or she is discharged, you should consider hiring an attorney or otherwise aplying pressure. You might try writing to your spouse's Commanding Officer, Chaplain, or the base Psychologist, explaining your situation and asking that he or she discuss the problem with your spouse.

Assuming that your spouse is agreeable to being divorced, **and is stationed in the United States,** service is made as follows:

STEP 1 - Prepare the Divorce Complaint, Summons and Child Custody Affidavit (if one is necessary) as usual.

STEP 2 - Prepare an Agreement and Waiver form (see Form 22). While you should model your form after Form 22, be sure to make the changes necessary to reflect your own situation.

STEP 3 - Send a copy of the Divorce Complaint, a copy of the Divorce Summons, a copy of the Child Custody Affidavit (if one is necessary) and the original **and** one copy of the Agreement and Waiver to your spouse by certified mail. Be sure to write clearly on the envelope, "Certified Mail Restricted Delivery, Return Receipt Requested."

Enclose a letter to your spouse asking that he or she sign the **original** of the Agreement and Waiver, have his or her signature notarized and return it to you as soon as possible. Your spouse can keep the **copy** of the Agreement and Waiver for his or her records.

STEP 4 - Within a short time you should receive a green return receipt card back in the mail proving that the certified letter was received by your spouse. Prepare an Affidavit of Service (see Form 13) and staple the green return receipt card to it.

STEP 5 - As soon as you have completed Step 4, file the following papers with the court clerk:

A. the original Divorce Complaint;

B. the original Divorce Summons;
C. your Affidavit of Service with green card attached, and
D. a Child Custody Affidavit (if one is necessary)

STEP 6 - As soon as you receive the signed and notarized Agreement and Waiver form from your spouse, file this with the clerk too. Your divorce can be heard sixty days after the day your spouse was served with papers, as in all other divorce cases. But, you must file the Agreement and Waiver form with the clerk before the actual hearing date.

STEP 7 - You should not file a Federal Affidavit when divorcing a spouse who is in the military service.

If your spouse is stationed overseas, judges often insist that personal service be made on him or her. In this case, prepare the Divorce Complaint, Summons, Child Custody Affidavit (if one is necessary) and the Agreement and Waiver as described above. Follow the directions for service-in-hand described in **Section a** of this chapter, using your spouse's Commanding Officer to make service instead of a sheriff. Ask the Commanding Officer to fill in the appropriate sections of the Summons indicating that service has been made and return it to you along with the notarized Agreement and Waiver for filing.

e. Service in a Foreign Country

Even if your spouse is a citizen of another country or is living there when you decide to get a divorce, you can get a divorce in Maine, so long as **you** meet one of the jurisdictional requirements described in Chapter 3.

Service on a spouse in a foreign country can be done in several ways, but in a **pro se** divorce, there are two easy ways:

1. **Delivery in hand by an adult other than yourself:** Have the Complaint and Summons (and Child Custody Affidavit, if necessary) delivered to your spouse **personally** by someone 18 years of age or older. You cannot do this yourself, but any other adult can. The person making service must hand all the necessary papers to your spouse personally and then must write the location and date when service was completed on the original Summons. In other words, that adult must fill in the Summons completely, just as if he or she was a deputy sheriff, and then return the original form to you to be filed with the court.

2. **Certified Mail:** By any form of mail requiring a signed receipt (certified or registered) **to be addressed and dispatched by the Clerk of Courts** to the person to be served. Proof of service shall include a receipt signed by your spouse or other evidence of delivery "satisfactory to the Court." Because the "return receipt" will be mailed to the court clerk, you should check with him or her to find out when it is returned. This is necessary for you to know when you can set the hearing date.

If neither of these methods work for you, you should consult an attorney.

FORM 12 SHERIFF'S LETTER, PERSONAL SERVICE

(sample form letter to Sheriff)

Back Road
Freeport, Maine 04032

July 6, 1988

Deputy Ronald Smith
7 Oak Street
Bar Harbor, Maine 04609

Re: Brown v. Brown

Dear Deputy Smith:

Enclosed you will find the original Summons and one copy of the Complaint and Summons (and Child Custody Affidavit if one is necessary) for the Divorce in the above entitled case. I am forwarding these papers to you for service upon the Defendant, John D. Brown.

The Defendant can be served at 370 Main Street in Bar Harbor, his residence. He is usually there after 7:00 p.m. at night. He works at the Happy Day Fish Factory, also on Main Street in Bar Harbor and is usually there between 7:00 a.m. and 4:00 p.m.

Please be assured that upon receipt of the executed papers from your office, your bill will be promptly paid.

Thank you for your assistance in this matter.

Sincerely,

Susan T. Brown

Enclosures:

Copy of Complaint
One original and one copy of Summons for Divorce
Copy of Uniform Child Custody Affidavit (if necessary)

FORM 13 AFFIDAVIT OF SERVICE

STATE OF MAINE
Cumberland, ss

DISTRICT COURT
District Eight
Division of Eastern
Cumberland
Civil Action Docket No.

SUSAN T. BROWN of Freeport, County of Cumberland, State of Maine, Plaintiff	
-vs-	AFFIDAVIT OF SERVICE
JOHN D. BROWN of Hungry Horse, County of Flathead, State of Montana, Defendant	

I, Susan T. Brown did, on July 5, 1988, mail by Certified Mail, Return Receipt Requested, Restricted Delivery, a copy of the attached Complaint for Divorce, Divorce Summons, and Child Custody Affidavit to the Defendant, Mr. John D. Brown, addressed as follows:

"Mr. John D. Brown
Sweet Grass Road
Hungry Horse, Montana 59919."

Attached hereto and incorporated herein by reference is the original receipt showing delivery of said aforementioned letter to Mr. John D. Brown on July 9, 1988.

Dated: July 14, 1988

____
Susan T. Brown

STATE OF MAINE
Cumberland, ss

Personally appeared the above named ____________________ and made oath that the foregoing statements by him/her voluntarily signed are true.

____
Notary Public

FORM 14 AFFIDAVIT OF SERVICE - REFUSED LETTER

STATE OF MAINE	DISTRICT COURT
	District Eight
CUMBERLAND, ss.	Division of Eastern Cumberland
	Civil Action
	Docket No. ______________________

* * * * * * * * * * * * * * * *

SUSAN T. BROWN of Freeport, County of Cumberland, State of Maine, *

Plaintiff *

-vs- * AFFIDAVIT OF SERVICE

JOHN D. BROWN of Bar Harbor, County of Flathead, State of Montana, *

Defendant *

* * * * * * * * * * * * * * * *

I, Susan T. Brown did, on July 5, 1988, mail by Certified Mail, Return Receipt Requested, Restricted Delivery, a copy of the attached Complaint for Divorce, Divorce Summons, and Child Custody Affidavit to the Defendant, Mr. John D. Brown, addressed as follows:

"Mr. John D. Brown
Sweet Grass Road
Hungry Horse, Montana 59919"

Attached hereto and incorporated herein by reference is the original envelope which shows that acceptance was refused. On July 9, 1988, I mailed the Complaint, Summons and Child Custody Affidavit to the Defendant at the same address by regular mail.

Dated:____________________ ______________________________
Plaintiff, Pro Se

(CONTINUED ON NEXT PAGE)

STATE OF MAINE

CUMBERLAND, ss.

Personally appeared the above named ______________________

and made oath that the foregoing statements by him/her voluntarily signed are true.

____

Notary Public

FORM 15 MOTION FOR SERVICE BY PUBLICATION

STATE OF MAINE

DISTRICT COURT
District Eight
Division of Eastern
Cumberland
Civil Action,
Docket No.____________

* * * * * * * * * * * * * * * * * * *

SUSAN T. BROWN, Plaintiff -vs- JOHN D. BROWN, Defendant	MOTION FOR SERVICE BY PUBLICATION

* * * * * * * * * * * * * * * * * * *

PURSUANT TO Rule 4(g) of the Maine Rules of Civil Procedure, Plaintiff moves for Service by Publication in that the address of the Defendant is unknown and cannot be ascertained by reasonable diligence; and Defendant cannot with due diligence be served by any other prescribed method. Any real or personal property of the Defendant in Cumberland County is at issue.

WHEREFORE, Plaintiff respectfully requests this Court to order Service by Publication in the Bath-Brunswick Times Record for three successive weeks.

Dated:__________________

____
Plaintiff, pro se

STATE OF MAINE

DISTRICT COURT
District Eight
Division of Eastern
Cumberland
Civil Action,
Docket No.____________

* * * * * * * * * * * * * * * * * * *
SUSAN T. BROWN of Freeport, County of Cumberland, State of Maine,

<u>Plaintiff</u>

-vs-

JOHN D. BROWN of Parts Unknown,

<u>Defendant</u>
* * * * * * * * * * * * * * * * * * *

<u>AFFIDAVIT IN SUPPORT OF</u>

<u>MOTION FOR SERVICE</u>

<u>BY PUBLICATION</u>

Now comes Susan T. Brown, Plaintiff in the above entitled action, and being duly sworn, states as follows:

1. I have not seen, heard from, or had any contact with my spouse, John D. Brown, since approximately September 22nd, 1979.

2. I have been searching for my spouse since April 15, 1981.

3. This search has involved attempts to contact my spouse, John D. Brown, by certified U.S. mail:

(a) at his last known address, 4 Front Street, Bar Harbor, Maine;

(b) in care of his mother, Naomi S. Brown, at 18 Reed Street, Missoula, Montana;

(c) in care of his sister, Rebecca Stevens, at RFD #2, Cuba, New Mexico.

4. On May 1st, 1981 I telephoned 406-324-9046, which is the telephone number of my spouse's mother and she refused to give me

(CONTINUED ON NEXT PAGE)

any information about the whereabouts of my spouse.

5. I do not know the whereabouts of my spouse.

Dated: July 22, 1988 ____________________________

Susan T. Brown, Plaintiff

STATE OF MAINE
Cumberland, ss

Personally appeared the above named ____________________________ and made oath that the foregoing statements by him/her voluntarily signed are true.

Dated: ________________ ____________________________

Notary Public

FORM 17 ORDER FOR SERVICE BY PUBLICATION

STATE OF MAINE

DISTRICT COURT
District Eight
Division of Eastern
Cumberland
Civil Action,
Docket No.____________

* * * * * * * * * * * * * * * * * * * *

SUSAN T. BROWN of Freeport, County of Cumberland, State of Maine,

Plaintiff

-vs-

JOHN D. BROWN of Parts Unknown,

Defendant

* * * * * * * * * * * * * * * * * * * *

ORDER FOR SERVICE BY PUBLICATION

THIS Court has heard the Motion of Susan T. Brown, Plaintiff, whose address is Back Road, Freeport, Maine, for Service by Publication upon Defendant, John D. Brown, pursuant to Maine Civil Court Rule 4(g). This is an action for divorce brought by the Plaintiff, Susan T. Brown, against her spouse, John D. Brown, and that all of the real and personal property of the Defendant in Cumberland County is at issue; and that the address of the Defendant is not known and cannot be ascertained by reasonable diligence; and that the Defendant cannot with due diligence be served by any other prescribed method; it is

ORDERED that the Defendant appear and serve an Answer to the Complaint on the Plaintiff at her said address on or before the ______ day of __________________,

19____, A.D.

(CONTINUED ON NEXT PAGE)

THE DEFENDANT IS NOTIFIED THAT IF HE FAILS TO DO SO, JUDGMENT BY DEFAULT MAY BE TAKEN AGAINST HIM FOR THE RELIEF GRANTED IN THE COMPLAINT. His Answer should also be filed with the Eighth District Court, Division of Eastern Cumberland, 28 Federal Street, Brunswick, Maine 04011.

IT IS FURTHER ORDERED that this order be published in the Bath-Brunswick Times Record, a daily newspaper published at Brunswick, Maine, once a week for three successive weeks, first publication to be made on or before ____________________________.

Dated:____________________

____
JUDGE, Eighth District Court

A TRUE COPY

ATTEST:________________________
Clerk

FORM 18

PETITION AND ORDER FOR MILITARY CERTIFICATION

STATE OF MAINE

CUMBERLAND County
(Indicate County Where Issued)

District Court
Division of Eastern Cumberland
Location Brunswick, Maine
Docket Number ______

SUSAN T. BROWN *Plaintiff*

vs.

JOHN D. BROWN *Defendant*

PETITION AND ORDER FOR MILITARY CERTIFICATION

RESPECTFULLY REPRESENTS Susan T. Brown of Freeport in the County of Cumberland and State of Maine thatshe married John D. Brown of Parts Unknown at Bangor in the County of Penobscot and State of Maine on July 14, 1969.

That it is impossible to ascertain by reasonable diligence the whereabouts of the said John D. Brown whose date of birth October 20, 1941, Social Security number 006-36-3491, service number unknown and other identifying characteristics are as follows: The Defendant is 6' tall and has brown hair and brown eyes

WHEREFORE IT IS RESPECTFULLY REQUESTED that this Honorable Court will issue an Order to the Adjutant General of the United States Army; Chief of Staff, United States Air Force, Washington, D.C.; the Chief, Bureau of Naval Personnel, Department of the Navy, Washington, D.C.; Commandant, United States Marine Corps, Washington, D.C.; and to the Commandant, United States Coast Guard, Headquarters, Washington, D.C., directing them to issue certificates as provided for by Section 601 of the Soldiers and Sailors Civil Relief Act of 1940.

______
Plaintiff

Address reply to: Susan T. Brown, Back Road, Freeport, Maine 04032

ORDER

Upon the foregoing Petition and after a hearing, it is hereby ORDERED, ADJUDGED AND DECREED that attested copies of said Petition and of the Order issue to the Adjutant General of the United States Army; Chief of Staff, United States Air Force, Washington, D.C.; the Chief, Bureau of Naval Personnel, Department of the Navy, Washington, D.C.; Commandant, United States Marine Corps, Washington, D.C.; and to the Commandant, United States Coast Guard, Headquarters, Washington, D.C., directing them to issue certificates provided for by Section 601 of the Soldiers and Sailors Civil Relief Act of 1940.

______
Judge of District Court

DCCV-23 Rev. (1/83)

FORM 19 SAMPLE LETTER TO NEWSPAPER REQUESTING PUBLICATION

July 22, 1988

Bath-Brunswick Times Record
Industry Road
Brunswick, Maine 04011

Re: Brown v. Brown

To Whom It May Concern:

I am forwarding to you the Order for Service by Publication in the above entitled matter to be published in your newspaper for three successive weeks, first publication to commence on or before _____________________ (fill in the date specified on the judge's Order).

When this has been completed, would you please complete the enclosed verification, have it notarized, and return it to me, along with a tear sheet showing the actual publication.

Sincerely,

Susan T. Brown

FORM 20 VERIFICATION OF PUBLICATION

STATE OF MAINE
Cumberland, ss

I,______________________________, being duly sworn, depose and say, that I am an employee of the _______(name of newspaper)____, a _____(daily or weekly)__________newspaper of general circulation in _______________________ County, Maine; that the order of service by publication in the matter of Brown v. Brown, of which the attached clipping is a copy, was published in said newspaper once a week for three successive weeks; and that the first publication was made in the issue of _____________________, 19__.

STATE OF MAINE,

Cumberland, ss.

Personally appeared the above named _________________________ and made oath that the foregoing statements by him/her voluntarily signed are true.

Dated:____________________

____
Notary Public

FORM 21 LETTER REQUESTING ARMED SERVICE CERTIFICATE

(date)

Chief of Navy Personnel
PERS-17-NMPC-03
Navy Department
Naval Military Personnel Command
Washington, D.C. 20370-5000

RE: John D. Brown
Social Security No. 003-49-0004 (if known)
Date of Birth: April 4, 1950

Gentlemen:

Would you please supply me with an Armed Service Certificate for the above individual. I have enclosed an Order for Military Search, signed by Judge Reed.

An action for divorce is now pending between the parties in the Maine District Court, District 8, Division of Eastern Cumberland. I am unable to ascertain by reasonable diligence the whereabouts of the said John D. Brown. His last known address was 5 Front Street, Bar Harbor, Maine.

Very truly yours,

Susan T. Brown

Enclosures:

Order for Military Search
Check for $5.20

FORM 22 **AGREEMENT AND WAIVER (MILITARY SERVICE)**

STATE OF MAINE

DISTRICT COURT
Division of Eastern Cumberland
Location: Brunswick, Maine
DOCKET NO.__________________

* * * * * * * * * * * * * * * * *
SUSAN T. BROWN *
<u>Plaintiff</u> *
-vs- *
JOHN D. BROWN *
<u>Defendant</u>
* * * * * * * * * * * * * * * * *

<u>AGREEMENT AND WAIVER</u>

In the matter of the above-entitled divorce action, commenced or to be commenced against me by my wife, Susan T. Brown, I, John D. Brown, hereby state that I do not wish to contest the divorce itself and I further agree that:

1. My wife, Susan T. Brown, shall have sole parental rights and responsibilities for our two children, Margaret A. and Nathan J. Brown.

2. I will pay a reasonable sum of support for the said children.

3. My wife, Susan T. Brown, shall have sole title to our 1976 Fort Mustang automobile.

4. On the condition that my wife, Susan T. Brown, not seek attorney's fees or court costs for any action for divorce commenced against me, I do further agree to waive rights I may

(CONTINUED ON NEXT PAGE)

have under the Soldier's and Sailor's Civil Relief Act.

Dated: July 21, 1988

____
John D. Brown, Defendant

STATE OF MAINE
Hancock, ss.

Personally appeared before me the above named John D. Brown on this 21st day of July, 1988 and executed the above Agreement and Waiver of his own free will.

____
Notary Public

Chapter 12

File the Papers

As soon as your papers have been served, they are ready for "filing". Filing means taking the completed papers to the District court **where either you or your spouse lives** and handing them to the clerk to be placed in his or her files. To find out which court that is, match up the town you want to use with the corresponding court in the Court and County Locator at the end of this manual.

Filing your divorce complaint will cost $50.00 (at this time), unless the court has given you permission to do your divorce without cost. (You may want to read about the Application to Proceed In Forma Pauperis, described more fully in Chapter 10).

If you want to proceed without cost, you should first file your completed papers and your Application to Proceed In Forma Pauperis with the clerk and ask that the judge rule on your Application. After the judge has reviewed it, you should get a copy of your application back in the mail, with the judge's decision granting or denying your request on the bottom. If your request to proceed without cost is granted, you will be all set. If your request is denied, you should immediately pay the $50.00 fee to the court.

It is important to be certain that you give the clerk **all** of the necessary papers. Refer to the following chart to be sure.

A. In the case of **in-hand service** (by a sheriff) you will have the following papers to file:

1. The original of the Divorce Complaint;
2. The original of the Divorce Summons with the Sheriff's notes on it;
3. The original of the Child Custody Affidavit (if one is necessary);

B. In the case of service by **certified mail** you will have the following papers to file:

1. The original of the Divorce Complaint;
2. The original of the Divorce Summons;
3. The original of the Child Custody Affidavit (if one is necessary);
4. The Affidavit of Service with the green certified mail return receipt card attached.

If your spouse is in the military service or you do not know where he or she is, refer to the sections of Chapter 11, describing how service is made in these situations for filing instructions as well.

Be sure to file your papers at the Court within twenty (20) days of the date of service. If you do not do this, service must be made over again.

Chapter 13

Mediation

Since 1983, Maine law has required **couples with children who cannot agree on some aspect of the divorce (custody, property, etc.)** to go to court-ordered mediation. The only exception to this requirement is for "extraordinary cause shown" and this exception is discussed below.

Every District Court is assigned two or more mediators who have been trained to work with divorcing couples. The idea of this mediation is that divorcing couples can talk about their disagreements with a neutral third person, who can help them reach agreements on as many issues as possible.

Once it becomes obvious that you and your spouse are not going to be able to agree to every aspect of the divorce, either you or your spouse can write to the court and request mediation. The fee for this service is currently $100.00 (If you filed an Affidavit in Forma Pauperis which was granted by the Court, then you do not have to pay this fee.) The sample letter below is a request for the Court to set up mediation. (Form 23).

FORM 23 REQUEST FOR MEDIATION LETTER

March 17, 1988

Jane Smith, Clerk
Maine District Court
Anytown, Maine 04953

Re: Susan T. Brown v. John D. Brown

Dear Ms. Smith:

I would like to request that mediation be scheduled in this case as soon as possible. I have enclosed a check for $60.00 to cover this cost. (Or, if appropriate, "The mediation fee has been waived by the Court.").

Thank you for your attention to this matter.

Sincerely,

Susan T. Brown

It is a good idea to request mediation as soon as you believe that it will be necessary, because there may be a long waiting period in some courts. It is a good idea to set aside two or three hours for the first mediation session; if necessary, the parties can usually return to mediation for no additional cost. As this book goes to print, there are no courts in which mediation is scheduled in the evening.

You should bring completed Affidavits of Income and Assets and Child Support Worksheets to the mediation session. If you have had trouble figuring out these forms, bring them to mediation together with all the information needed to fill them out and ask the mediator for help.

If you and your spouse are able to reach an agreement with the help of the mediator, one of you should take responsibility for writing this agreement in a form which can be presented to the court. The draft Divorce Agreement which is provided in Chapter 14 can be used for this purpose. Both you and your spouse must sign the agreement and present it to the judge for approval as part of the final divorce order.

You and your spouse are required by law to mediate "in good faith." This means that you must really try to work things out through this process. If the Court finds that either you or your spouse did **not** mediate "in good faith," the Court could require you to return to mediation, or impose some other sanction. If the Court finds that **you** have not mediated in good faith, you should request that the Court allow time for you to find a lawyer to represent you. However, as long as you keep an open mind about the mediation process, the judge is very unlikely to find you have not mediated in good faith.

While mediation is a way to help you and your spouse work things out,it is not intended to keep you from going to court if you and your spouse cannot agree. If it becomes apparent that there are one or more issues on which you can't agree, then you should consider getting a lawyer to help you with the contested divorce hearing.

There is one exception to the requirement of mediation in contested cases with children. This is a recent addition to the law, and permits the judge to waive the mediation requirement "for extraordinary cause, supported by affidavit." One possible reason you might want to use this exception is if you are a battered spouse. Often, battered spouses are not able to successfully defend their needs in a hostile negotiation with their abuser. In fact, in the worst cases, a mediation session could expose the battered spouse to direct physical harm.

If you feel that the history of your relationship with your spouse is such that he or she presents a direct threat to you in the context of mediation, you should ask the judge to waive this requirement and attach an affidavit which lists the precise reasons you feel mediation is not possible. There is no court form for this Affidavit. You will have to make up your own. Your Affidavit should probably contain the same kinds of specific information listed in the "Affidavit For Temporary Relief From Abuse" (which is available as a form from the court clerk.) You can consult with the staff of an abused or battered women's project (see the list in Chapter 8) or a lawyer for help with this Affidavit. It is best to be as specific and detailed as possible, since it is up to you to persuade the judge that mediation would be very harmful in your case.

For more information about the mediation process generally, you can obtain a free pamphlet from the District Court nearest you.

Chapter 14

The Divorce Agreement

Many spouses find that the easiest way to make sure they have covered every issue in their divorce is by writing an agreement which both parties sign. This is called a "divorce agreement" and it is commonly used in divorces to show that a couple has been able to make decisions about all the major areas affected by the divorce. But, you do not have to have a divorce agreement to get a divorce. And, it does not take the place of the property list (described in Chapter 10) which must be submitted whether or not you have a divorce agreement.

On the next four pages, we have reproduced a divorce agreement which may be used by divorcing couples with different kinds of needs. You can photocopy this agreement and use it in your divorce. **But, be sure you cross out any sections which do not apply to the agreement that you and your spouse have made.** A sample completed form follows as Form 24, with a blank form following that.

Do not use this Agreement if you have negotiated a specific visitation schedule for the children, if you want to assign some but not all, parenting rights and responsibilities to one parent, if your real estate and other marital property is extensive or if you have any concerns that are not included in this agreement. This is only intended for very simple and clear cut agreements between you and your spouse. If your situation is more complicated, you will probably want to have a lawyer help you prepare your divorce agreement.

Be sure that both you and your spouse have signed the agreement.

If you and your spouse have made a divorce agreement, bring it to court with you on the day of your hearing and present it to the judge when you testify.

SAMPLE FORM 24 -- DIVORCE AGREEMENT

This Agreement has been entered into on August 3, 19 88 by Susan T. Brown (who will be referred to as the "Wife" in this agreement) and by John D. Brown (who will be referred to as the "Husband" in this agreement).

There is a pending action for divorce in District Court located in Brunswick (town), Cumberland (county), Maine. The divorce was filed by the wife/~~husband~~.

The parties have considered all relevant factors in reaching this agreement, which they both agree is fair, and they would like this agreement to be part of the final divorce order.

Ground for Divorce

1. The husband and wife agree that there are irreconcilable marital differences between them and that the marriage has completely broken down.

Child Custody and Support

1. The husband and wife have children under 18 years of age, named Margaret A. Brown d/o/b April 1, 1980
Nathan J. Brown d/o/b November 9, 1982
Sally J. Brown d/o/b May 5, 1983
Mary P. Brown d/o/b October 10, 1988

~~2. The husband and wife will share parental rights and responsibilities as to these minor children, but the children will live with ____________________. The parent who is not living with the children will have the right to visit with and be visited by the children at all reasonable and proper times.~~

~~or 2. The husband will have sole parental rights and responsibilities for the minor children, and the children will live with him. The wife will have the right to visit with and be visited by the children at all reasonable and proper times.~~

~~or~~ 2. The wife will have sole parental rights and responsibilities for the minor children, and the children will live with her. The husband will have the right to visit with and be visited by the children at all reasonable and proper times.

3. The parent who is not living with the children will pay __$20.00__ per week/~~month~~ as child support for each child.

4. The husband/~~wife~~ will be responsible for maintaining health insurance for the minor children and shall be responsible for all uninsured reasonable medical, dental, optical and hospital expenses for the minor children.

5. Husband and wife will have equal and full access to all medical and school records for the minor children.

Property

6. There is real estate which is marital property. It is located in __Freeport__, in __Cumberland__ County, Maine. The deed for this property is recorded in Book __4449__, __34__, in the __Cumberland__ County Registry of Deeds. The husband and wife intend for the ~~husband~~/wife to receive clear title to this property. The ~~husband~~/wife will execute the necessary papers to accomplish this (including the real estate abstract of divorce decree) within 10 days of the date of the divorce.

7. The following items of marital property will be awarded to the husband: Pioneer Stereo System; 1978 Saab Stationwagon; and

all other property now in the possession of John D. Brown

___.

8. The following items of marital property will be awarded to the wife: 1976 Red Ford Mustang; Color TV and VCR; and all other property now in the possession of Susan T. Brown

___.

9. All other items of property are personal in nature. The husband will keep those items of property which are currently in his possession and the wife will keep those items of property which are currently in her possession.

10. The following marital debts will be paid by the husband:

Sears Credit Card - $1,280.00

Mastercard - $920.00

___.

The following marital debts will be paid by the wife: ___

Coastal Lumber Company - $230.39

___.

11. Neither husband nor wife seeks alimony from the other.

12. The wife wishes to change her name to Susan Temple

___.

August 3, 1988 ________________________
Wife

August 3, 1988 ________________________
Husband

FORM 24 -- DIVORCE AGREEMENT

This Agreement has been entered into on ____________, 19___ by ______________________ (who will be referred to as the "Wife" in this agreement) and by _________________________ (who will be referred to as the "Husband" in this agreement).

There is a pending action for divorce in District Court located in _________________, ____________________, Maine. The
town County
divorce was filed by the wife/husband.

The parties have considered all relevant factors in reaching this agreement, which they both agree is fair, and they would like this agreement to be part of the final divorce Order.

Ground for Divorce

1. The husband and wife agree that there are irreconcilable marital differences between them and that the marriage has completely broken down.

Child Custody and Support

1. The husband and wife have children under 18 years of age, named ____________________________ d/o/b ___________________

_______________________________________ d/o/b ____________________

_______________________________________ d/o/b ____________________

2. The husband and wife will share parental rights and responsibilities as to these minor children, but the children will live with _______________________________. The parent who is not living with the children will have the right to visit with and be visited by the children at all reasonable and proper times.

or 2. The Husband will have sole parental rights and responsibilities for the minor children, and the children will live with him. The wife will have the right to visit with and be visited by the children at all reasonable and proper times.

or 2. The Wife will have sole parental rights and responsibilities for the minor children, and the children will live with her. The husband will have the right to visit with and be visited by the children at all reasonable and proper times.

3. The parent who is not living with the children will pay _____________ per week/month as child support for each child.

4. The husband/wife will be responsible for maintaining health insurance for the minor children and shall be responsible for all uninsured reasonable medical, dental, optical and hospital expenses for the minor children.

5. Husband and wife will have equal and full access to all medical and school records for the minor children.

Property

6. There is real estate which is marital property. It is located in _______________, in______________ County, Maine. The deed for this property is recorded in Book _______________, Page ____, in the __________ County Registry of Deeds. The husband and wife intend for the husband/wife to receive clear title to this property. The husband/wife will execute the necessary papers to
accomplish this (including the real estate abstract of divorce decree) within 10 days of the date of the divorce.

7. The following items of marital property will be awarded to the husband:____

____

____.

8. The following items of marital property will be awarded to the wife:____

____

____.

9. All other items of property are personal in nature. The Husband will keep those items of property which are currently in his possession and the Wife will keep those items of property which are currently in her possession.

10. The following marital debts will be paid by the Husband:____

____

____.

The following marital debts will be paid by the Wife:_______

____

____.

11. Neither Husband nor Wife seeks alimony from the other.

12. The Wife wishes to change her last name to ______________ ____.

______________________________ date

______________________________ Wife

______________________________ date

______________________________ Husband

Chapter 15

Prepare for the Divorce Hearing

a. The Waiting Period

There is a sixty-day waiting period between the date of service and the earliest time that your hearing can be held. Everyone has to wait this length of time — there's no getting around it (even if you're represented by a lawyer).

In counting off your sixty days, the date of service is not counted. So, if your spouse was served on April 6th, your sixty days begin to run on April 7th. Take out a calendar and count your sixty days — that's the simplest and easiest way to make sure that you are accurate:

☐ date of service

AUGUST

S	M	T	W	T	F	S
	1	2	3	[4]	~~5~~	~~6~~
~~7~~	~~8~~	~~9~~	~~10~~	~~11~~	~~12~~	~~13~~
~~14~~	~~15~~	~~16~~	~~17~~	~~18~~	~~19~~	~~20~~
~~21~~	~~22~~	~~23~~	~~24~~	~~25~~	~~26~~	~~27~~
~~28~~	~~29~~	~~30~~	~~31~~			

SEPTEMBER

S	M	T	W	T	F	S
				~~1~~	~~2~~	~~3~~
~~4~~	~~5~~	~~6~~	~~7~~	~~8~~	~~9~~	~~10~~
~~11~~	~~12~~	~~13~~	~~14~~	~~15~~	~~16~~	~~17~~
~~18~~	~~19~~	~~20~~	~~21~~	~~22~~	~~23~~	~~24~~
~~25~~	~~26~~	~~27~~	~~28~~	~~29~~	~~30~~	

OCTOBER

S	M	T	W	T	F	S
						~~1~~
~~2~~	~~3~~	[4]	5	6	7	8
9	10	11	12	13	14	15
16	17	18	19	20	21	22
23	24	25	26	27	28	29
30	31					

☐ the first day that you are eligible to go to court

Remember, the sixty days are not up until **after** the 60th day has passed. The waiting period is a good time to collect your thoughts and to start thinking about your hearing.

b. Set a Court Date

In most areas of Maine it is necessary to set a specific court date for your divorce hearing. This is done by going to the clerk's office and arranging a date on his or her hearing calendar. This will be the day that you appear in court for your divorce hearing.

c. Notify Your Spouse

Although not required by law, many judges require that your spouse be notified of the date set for the divorce hearing. Some will even refuse to hear your case on the scheduled day if your spouse hasn't had notice. (Of course, if your spouse filed an "Answer," you **must** notify him or her of the hearing).

It is strongly recommended that you send your spouse a certified letter in advance of the hearing, specifying the date set for the hearing. Make a copy of the letter and bring it and the return receipt from that certified letter to court with you. You need not show this to the judge unless he or she asks you about notification of your spouse. (If you can't afford to send the letter by certified mail, send it by ordinary mail. Be sure the date that you mailed it is clearly marked on the letter and make a copy of it to bring to court with you).

Your spouse does not need to be at the hearing and you may want to mention that in the letter to avoid any confusion.

d. Notify the Department of Human Services

If you checked on your complaint that you or your spouse are receiving public assistance, have received it in the past, or may receive it in the future, you must notify the Department of Human Services of the date set for your hearing.

Send a certified letter to the Department several days in advance of the hearing specifying the date set for the hearing. Make a copy of that letter and bring it, and the return receipt from the certified letter, to court with you. You need not show this to the judge unless he or she asks for it. (If you can't afford to send the letter by certified mail, send it by ordinary mail. Be sure the date that you mailed it is clearly marked on the letter and make a copy of it to bring to court with you).

e. Property List

You must file your property list **at least 3 days** before your divorce hearing. As we discussed in Chapter 10, you and your spouse can file separate lists or one joint list.

f. Child Support Affidavits and Worksheet

You must file your own affidavit and worksheet at least 3 days before your divorce hearing. Your spouse should also file these forms with the court 3 days before the hearing. However, if he or she does not file the affidavit, the judge will make a decision based on the available information.

g. Divorce Agreement

Although this is not required, it is helpful for the judge to have a divorce agreement which both the husband and wife have signed. This agreement can cover every aspect of the divorce, as discussed earlier in Chapter 14. Bring the divorce agreement to court with you on the day of the hearing and present it to the judge with your testimony.

h. Federal Affidavit

This should be filed either on the day of the hearing, or as close to that date as possible. You should prepare the form in advance and then bring it to a notary public to witness your signature. **Do not sign the Affidavit until you are in the presence of the Notary Public.** The court clerk is also a notary public, and may be willing to witness this form for you. Be sure to check with the clerk before the hearing to see if this can be arranged. Make sure that you have the correct information about your spouse's whereabouts on the Affidavit. If there is a chance that he or she has moved since being served with the Complaint, you should list the new address on the Affidavit.

i. Witnesses? Not Anymore

People may tell you that you will need tô bring two witnesses to court with you to testify that what you say is true. **You don't.** Maine law used to require witnesses but does not anymore.

However, if you are asking the court to order something unusual, such as extremely limited visitation, you may want to bring a witness with you. In the event that the judge is reluctant to make such an order, it would be useful to be able to "call" a witness to speak to the judge in court about the need for such an order, based on his or her own personal knowledge.

You may also want to bring a friend to court with you just for support. That's fine, and probably a good idea.

j. Court Watching

Court watching simply means going to the court and watching and listening to what happens there. It can serve an important purpose for you — to make you familiar with the courtroom procedure so that you will feel more comfortable on the day of your hearing.

You may or may not have your hearing in front of the same judge that you observe on the day that you "court watch."

Ask the court clerk when divorces are being heard and sit in on some hearings. This will give you a good idea of what to expect at your own hearing.

k. Prepare Your Testimony

On the day of your hearing, it will be necessary to tell the judge certain facts about your marriage, why you want a divorce, and what you are requesting. This will be your "testimony." Based on what you say in this testimony, the judge will decide whether to grant your divorce and what to order with regard to custody, support, alimony, property, etc.

You should prepare your testimony a few days in advance of the hearing and practice it several times. You may want to take an outline of your testimony to court with you to be sure you cover everything. Many judges will object if a person reads his or her testimony word for word from a written statement. However, you should have no problem if you make occasional reference to a written outline of your testimony. Some judges don't require you to make a statement on your own at all but instead, ask a series of questions. If a judge does do the questioning, be sure that he or she doesn't miss any of the issues which you want considered. In most cases, however, you will be required to give testimony yourself without any help from the judge. This is the situation for which you should be prepared.

There are certain things that must be included in your testimony. These items should form the basis of your outline. They are:

* your name and address

* how long you have lived in Maine
* your spouse's name and address
* when and where you were married
* where you most recently lived together
* that you are asking the court for a divorce and the ground that you're using
* whether there have been any previous actions filed for divorce or annulment (if there were, what happened)
* that there has been no collusion between you and your spouse to obtain a divorce
* whether there are children from this relationship and if so, their names and ages
* what you want the court to order in addition to the divorce itself, including requests for:

  parental rights and responsibility

  child support (including the amount and the Conditional Order of Income Withholding)

  visitation (specify limitation, if any, and any good reasons to support it)

  division of marital property and bills (refer to property list)

  alimony

  restoration of a former name

(If you and your spouse have signed a divorce agreement, you should mention that and make sure that the court has a copy of it).

* restate your ground and give testimony supporting it
* what, if any, attempts you have made at reconciliation and that there is no hope of reconciliation

Two sample testimonies follow. In the first example, the plaintiff is using the ground of Irreconcilable Marital Differences, and in the second, Cruel and Abusive Treatment.

1. Sample Testimony 1. - Irreconcilable Marital Differences

"My name is Susan T. Brown and I am a resident of Freeport, Maine. I have lived in Freeport for three years. My husband John D. Brown, is a resident of Bar Harbor, Maine. We were married July 14, 1969 by a Justice of the Peace in Bangor, Maine. We lived together in Freeport for the last three years until our separation in November of 1987.

I am requesting a divorce on the ground of Irreconcilable Marital Differences.

Neither of us has ever filed for a divorce or annulment before. There has been no collusion between us to obtain a divorce.

My husband and I have three children from our marriage, Mary, who is 12, Nathan J., who is 9, and Sally who is 4. These children have been with me since our separation and they will live with me, but see their father every other weekend and during vacations and holidays. He and I want to share parental rights and responsibilities for them.

Both my husband and I have filed income affidavits with the court. I have also filed the child support worksheet. Based on these I believe he should pay $141 a week for all 3 children. I have prepared a Conditional Order of Income Withholding which I will now give you. I would like this order to be part of the final divorce judgment.

I have filed a property list and will now give you a divorce agreement signed by myself and my husband. I request that the terms of this agreement be included in my divorce order.

I am asking for a divorce on the ground of Irreconcilable Marital Differences. My husband and I finally separated approximately eleven months ago. We were just unable to live together any longer.

Beginning about three years ago, we began to have serious disagreements over several things. I wanted to go to work once the children were in school and he refused to allow me to do so. If he found out I had a job interview scheduled he would call the employer and tell him not to hire me.

John wanted to have more children and I didn't. I felt that I had my hands full with four and wanted to do a good job of raising them.

When the children disobeyed he would hit them. I don't believe in that type of punishment, but he ignored me.

We argued constantly about these problems. We just couldn't agree. I became terribly upset and depressed about these arguments.

We spoke with our priest several times trying to work out our problems but this didn't help either. Finally we both agreed that we could not get along and we separated.

I believe that we have tried everything possible to work out the problems in our marriage, but they just can't be resolved.

I have no further testimony but I would be glad to answer any questions."

Sample Testimony 2. — Cruel and Abusive Treatment

"My name is Susan T. Brown and I am a resident of Freeport, Maine. My husband, John D. Brown, is a resident of Bar Harbor, Maine. We were married on July 14th, 1979 by a Justice of the Peace in Bangor, Maine. We lived together in Freeport throughout our marriage until we separated in November of 1987.

Neither of us has ever filed for a divorce before. There has been no collusion between us to obtain a divorce.

I am asking for a divorce on the ground of Cruel and Abusive Treatment.

We have two children from our marriage, Mary who is 12, and Nathan John, who is 9. These children have been with me since our separation and I would like to have the court order sole parental rights and responsibility of them to me. I have filed the income affidavit for myself.

I don't think my husband filled one out. He earns around $25,000 a year at the local plant. I brought a paystub of his to prove it, and I have filled out the child support worksheet also. I am earning $8,000 per year and pay $40 a week for my youngest to be in day care. Based on this information, I am asking for child support of $139.00 per week. I have prepared a Conditional Order of Income Withholding which I will now give you. I would like this Order to be part of the final divorce judgment.

I have filed a property list. My husband and I have already divided our property and I would like the final divorce order to set aside to me, all the property which is now in my possession and set aside to my husband, all the property which is now in his possession.

I am asking the court to grant me a divorce on the ground of Cruel and Abusive Treatment for the following reasons:

After we had been married for about six years, we began to argue frequently. My husband drank a lot and he would yell at me for no reason after he had been drinking. Many times he would abuse me physically. He tried to make me have sexual relations with him when he was in this condition and wouldn't allow me to sleep if I refused. He insulted me in front of my friends and the children. He never did anything around the house and refused to help with even the simplest household chores. When he became unemployed, and refused to try to find another job, I had to go to work. He refused to care for the children while I worked, and I had to hire a babysitter for them.

Many times he would leave me home to spend time with friends and never invited me to come. Some nights he would never come home at all. I would worry about whether he had been hurt or if he had just left me.

As a result, I became extremely nervous. I took sleeping pills because I was often unable to sleep on the nights that he wouldn't come home. I started to lose weight and I had no interest in eating.

I tried to persuade him to go to a marriage counselor but he refused. He even refused to talk with his parents about the problems that we were having, although they offered to try to help.

I felt that if I continued to live with him I would become even more withdrawn and depressed."

We have included a variety of situations in the sample testimonies in order to give you an idea of the type of problems that might persuade a judge to grant a divorce. Your spouse need not be as difficult to live with as John No. 1 or as cruel as John No. 2, in order to show sufficient evidence to prove your ground. However, if you use Cruel and Abusive Treatment, you must be able to show the judge that you have really been mistreated and how that treatment affected you, or he or she may conclude that you should have used Irreconcilable Marital Differences.

Chapter 16

The Day of the Hearing

People are usually nervous about the idea of going to court. If you have read this manual carefully and feel well prepared, that should help. Perhaps bringing a friend to court with you might help too. If you think so, do it.

While courts no longer have a dress code, judges consider an appearance in their court to be a serious occasion and want people to dress respectfully.

You should plan to arrive at the courthouse about fifteen to twenty minutes early on the day of your hearing. This will give you plenty of time to check with the clerk and learn what the procedure will be. In some cases you must pick up your divorce file from the clerk and give it to the judge. In other cases, the clerk will give the file to the judge. The clerk will be able to explain whatever procedure is used to you so that things will run smoothly.

Be sure at this point that the judge has all of the papers that you want him or her to see. Make sure that you have filed the Federal Affidavit, the Property List, the Conditional Order of Income Withholding, and all papers necessary to show that you have made service correctly. Be sure to bring the copy of the letter you sent your spouse notifying him or her of the hearing and the return receipt proving it was sent. If you are required to notify the Department of Human Services, bring proof that you have. If you and your spouse have prepared a divorce agreement, be sure to bring that too.

When you walk into the courtroom itself, find a seat and wait until your case is called. Divorce cases are heard in open court and so there will probably be other people present. Most of them are probably there for a divorce too and are feeling much the way you are. However, if you are very nervous about speaking in front of strangers or if you want to testify about something very personal and private, **you have the right to ask the judge to exclude the public.** The judge must do this unless your spouse objects.

The judge will probably begin the hearing by directing you to take the stand and swearing you in. After this is done, you will begin your testimony. Although most people prefer to have an outline to refer to, you should be well enough prepared so that you will only need to look at this outline occasionally. Your presentation should last approximately three or five minutes unless the judge has questions to ask you.

If the judge does question you, don't assume that you have done something wrong. Repeat the question to yourself, ask yourself what the judge really wants to know and then answer it simply and directly. There is nothing unusual about a judge asking questions. He or she may not have heard something that you said, or may just want more detail. Judges will sometimes ask you why you want a particular order, especially if that order is in any way out of the ordinary (for example, restricted visitation). Do not be afraid to defend your need for such an order. The judge may just want to know how important and necessary the order is to you.

After all of the testimony has been presented and the judge has asked whatever questions he or she might have, you will usually be told whether or not your divorce has been granted and what orders will be made. If the judge neglects to make a particular order at this time, you should question him or her about it immediately. It is quite possible that he or she simply forgot the issue and needs to be reminded about it.

If the judge does not indicate at all how he or she will rule on your case, you can ask, or you can wait and speak with the clerk later.

Do not worry if the procedure in court has not followed exactly the model we have just described. In fact, watch the judge carefully for cues throughout the proceeding. This, however, will be the basic format and your hearing should not vary greatly from it.

a. Continuances

If there is a problem with your divorce papers or with the procedure you have followed, the judge will often continue the case rather than deny the divorce. The continuance will give you a chance to correct the error.

In fact, you can ask for a continuance yourself at any time during the hearing. If an issue is raised that you are not prepared for or you feel yourself getting into trouble for some other reason, it may be helpful to postpone things and collect your thoughts. Although the judge has the power to grant or deny your request for a continuance, he or she will most probably grant it.

If the judge calls for the continuance, he or she will usually tell you why. If not, you should ask.

You will usually be able to correct the problem yourself by following the judge's instructions or re-reading the manual. If you are unable to resolve the problem yourself, you should see a lawyer as soon as possible.

Once the problem has been resolved, you should call the clerk to reschedule the hearing. Notify your spouse (and the Department of Human Services, if necessary) of the new hearing date by certified mail. Things should go more smoothly this time.

b. What to do if Your Divorce Is Denied

If your divorce is denied (and this is very unlikely) you have two alternatives. They are:

1. An appeal to Superior Court.
2. Try again from the beginning.

Make sure that you understand exactly why your divorce was denied before making this decision.

If you decide to appeal, you must work very quickly as certain necessary parts of the appeal must be done within 10 days. You will need an attorney at this point, and should hire one **immediately.**

Your other alternative is to begin again. You may start the whole procedure over again, immediately if you like. You may want to use a different ground, or to try to schedule the hearing when a different judge is on the bench.

But, this is not to end on a note of pessimism. It is very rare that an uncontested divorce is actually denied. Read this manual carefully, take your time, and you should have no problem.

Chapter 17

After the Hearing

a. The Divorce Judgment

Once you have learned that your divorce will be granted, a "Judgment" must be prepared. The Divorce Judgment is a legal paper, signed by the judge, that contains the terms settled on during the divorce hearing.

In most courts, the clerk is responsible for preparing the Divorce Judgment. However, in some parts of the State, the person bringing the divorce action must also prepare the Judgment. Check with your local clerk before leaving the court on the day of the hearing to learn how this issue is handled in your area.

The court has two different pre-printed divorce judgment forms. In cases involving children, it will be easier to use the long form. Completed samples of both forms follow as Forms 25 (short form) and 26 (long form) and are also included in the Appendix.

If you do have to prepare your own Judgment, study the forms below. Make your judgment conform to the orders made in your particular case. The clerk will be able to tell you exactly what has been ordered if you are unsure.

Assuming that your spouse does not appeal the judge's order (and an appeal is very unlikely in most pro se divorces), the divorce will be final ten days after the judge signs the order. If you want the divorce to be effective immediately, you and your spouse each must sign a "Waiver of Appeal" form which the court clerk can provide after the hearing. This form says that neither one of you wants to appeal the judge's final order. You must return the signed form to the clerk; once you have done that, your divorce will be final.

The original of the Divorce Judgment goes into the file with the original of the Complaint and Summons to be kept by the court.

After ten days have passed, you can get an attested copy of the Judgment from the court clerk.

NOTE: If the judge makes an order in your case regarding child support, be sure to carefully include all of that order in your judgment. You may find that the judge orders a separate amount of support for each child, or that the amount changes when the child(ren) reach 12 or 18 years old. All of this should be specifically included in your final order.

The judge may also decide to order an amount of support that is different from the amount on the child support table. If so, you must write the judge's reasons for not using the amount in the child support table in the judgment.

If you are using the court's Divorce Judgment Long Form (Form 26), you may want to cross out all of the printed language at Paragraph 6 and replace it with new language that more accurately reflects the judge's order. If you do not have room on the printed page, simply write at Paragraph 6 "See Child Support Order Attached" and type it on a separate sheet of paper and attach it to your judgment.

STATE OF MAINE

District Court
Division of Eastern Cumberland
Location Brunswick, Maine
Docket No. ______

SUSAN BROWN *Plaintiff*

vs.

JOHN D. BROWN *Defendant*

DIVORCE JUDGMENT

Notice of the pendency of this action for divorce has been duly and seasonably given according to law. This action was heard before me and the allegations and the evidence were fully presented and considered. A divorce from the bonds of matrimony is hereby ORDERED and ADJUDGED to Susan T. Brown from John D. Brown for the cause of Irreconcilable marital differences

The counterclaim/complaint is dismissed.

It is further ordered and decreed that the property of each spouse is set apart to him or her*, and after consideration of all relevant factors including those listed at 19 M.R.S.A. § 722-A, the court hereby divides the marital property as follows:

To Susan T. Brown: 1. Land and Buildings located on Back Road in Freeport, County of Cumberland, State of Maine, and more fully described in a deed from Thomas and Marjorie Smith to the parties dated October 31, 1969 and filed at the Cumberland County Registry of Deeds, Book 4449, Page 34.

2. The parties' 1976 red Ford Mustang, serial number: XYZ-220-300-400A.

To John D. Brown: 1. The parties' 1978 Blue Saab Stationwagon, serial number: QRS-200-300-400Z.

It is further ordered and adjudged that the said Susan T. Brown assume full responsibility for the mortgage payments for the above described proeprty, beginning with the payment due September 1, 1988.

It is further ordered and adjudged that the said Susan T. Brown be responsible for preparing and recording a copy of this decree or an abstract thereof for filing at the Cumberland County Registry of Deeds and for paying all fees necessary therefor.

The clerk is directed to incorporate this judgment by reference in the docket for this case.

Dated:

____
District Court Judge

A true copy,

Attest:

____
(Deputy) Clerk

DCCV-17 Rev. (1/86)

*[If the judge does make a specific order regarding separate (non-marital) property, this paragraph should read:
"It is further ordered and decreed that the property of each spouse is set apart to him or her as follows:
To Susan Brown: a 16' wooden homemade skiff, Maine registration: ME 9046H
To John D. Brown: an antique gold pocket watch engraved with date 10/31/06.
And after consideration of all...(continue with example above"]

FORM 26.

STATE OF MAINE

DISTRICT COURT
Division Eastern Cumberland
Location Brunswick, Maine
Docket No. ______

SUSAN T. BROWN

Plaintiff

v.

JOHN D. BROWN

Defendant

DIVORCE JUDGMENT

1. Notice of this action for divorce has been given according to law. This action was heard before me, and the allegations and the evidence were fully presented and considered. A divorce from the bonds of matrimony is hereby ORDERED to ~~the~~ (~~parties~~) Susan T. Brown for the cause of ~~(~~irreconcilable marital differences~~)~~ ______.

☐ ~~2. It is further ORDERED that the terms of a settlement agreement between the parties, dated ______, are approved and incorporated herein.~~

☐ 3. With respect to their minor child(ren), namely Mary P. Brown, Margaret A. Brown, Nathan J. Brown and Sally J. Brown
it is ORDERED that ~~(allocated) (shared)~~ (sole) parental rights and responsibilities are awarded to Susan T. Brown as follows:

☐ 4. The right is given to John D. Brown to have contact with and by said child(ren) at all reasonable and proper times.

☐ ~~5. It is further ORDERED that ______ shall have reasonable rights of access to said child(ren).~~

☐ 6. It is further ORDERED that John D. Brown pay to Susan T. Brown the sum of $ 20.00 for each child per week toward the support of said child(ren), the first payment to be made ______, 19 ______, and payment shall be made to the State of Maine Department of Human Services for all periods that Susan T. Brown receives Aid to Dependent Children for such child(ren).

☐ 7. It is further ORDERED that John D. Brown maintain medical insurance for such child(ren) and pay Susan T. Brown all reasonable medical, hospital, optical and dental expenses for such child(ren).

☐ 8. It is further ORDERED that each parent shall have access to records and information pertaining to the child(ren), including, but not limited to, medical, dental and school records.

☐ ~~9. It is further ORDERED that ______ pay to ______ as alimony the sum of $______~~ ______.

DCCV-16 Rev. (1/86)

☐ 10. It is further ORDERED that the following property be set aside or awarded as follows:

To Susan T. Brown: 1. Land and Buildings located on Back Road in Freeport, County of Cumberland, State of Maine, and more fully described in a Deed from Thomas and Marjorie Smith to the Parties dated October 31, 1969 and filed at the Cumberland County Registry of Deeds, Book 4449, Page 34.

2. The Parties' 1982 red Ford Mustang, serial number: XYZ-200-300-400A.

To John D. Brown: 1. The Parties' 1979 green Dodge pick-up truck, serial number: QRS-200-300-400Z.

☐ 11. It is further ORDERED

that the said Susan T. Brown assume full responsibility for the mortgage payments for the above described property, beginning with the payment due September 1, 1988, and

that the said Susan T. Brown be responsible for preparing and recording a copy of this decree or an abstract thereof for filing at the Cumberland County Registry of Deeds and for paying all fees necessary therefor.

☐ 12. (Plaintiff) ~~(Defendant)~~ is granted the right to change her name to Susan Temple

~~☐ 13. It is further ORDERED that ______ pay to ______ the sum of $______ as counsel fees, execution to issue.~~

☐ 14. The clerk is directed to incorporate this judgment by reference in the docket book.

Date: ______________________

____
Judge, District Court

A true copy,
Attest:

____
(Deputy) Clerk

b. Real Estate Abstract of Divorce Decree

If you are going to be awarded real estate by the judge, you must prepare an abstract of your Divorce Judgment to be filed at the Registry of Deeds in the county in which the property is located. The abstract is a document signed and sealed by the clerk, certifying that you have been legally awarded the property by the court. It has the same effect as a quit-claim deed from your spouse releasing all of his or her interest in the property to you.

This form should be prepared as soon as the judge makes an order regarding property. If you are preparing the Divorce Judgment, you should prepare the real estate abstract at the same time. A blank court form is provided in the Appendix and a sample completed form is provided here as Form 27. Check with your District Court to make sure that the blank form Abstract is acceptable. If so, photocopy it and type in the missing information, as the example Abstract is done.

In order to complete the abstract form, you must use the exact wording from your Divorce Judgment regarding property. If you are preparing the Divorce Judgment yourself this should be no problem. However, if the clerk is preparing the Judgment, you should check with him or her immediately after the hearing to see when you can have access to that language.

The recording fee for the abstract is paid to the clerk of the court **before** the divorce becomes final. The clerk will send the abstract for recording to the registry of deeds by certified mail or by hand after the 10 day appeal period has gone by.

FORM 27.

STATE OF MAINE

SUPERIOR COURT	DISTRICT COURT
______________, ss.	Division of Eastern Cumberland
Docket No. ______________	Location Brunswick, Maine
	Docket No. ______________

ABSTRACT OF DIVORCE DECREE

I, Mamie R. Bilideau, the duly appointed, qualified and acting Clerk of the District Court, Eastern Cumberland ~~County~~/Division, hereby certify that on the 29th day of October, 19 88, a decree of divorce became final between Susan T. Brown, Plaintiff, of Freeport, Maine; and John D. Brown, Defendant, of Bar Harbor, Maine, and that the following is a true copy of so much of said decree as relates to the disposition or transfer of real estate in Cumberland County, Viz:

To Susan T. Brown: 1. Land and Buildings located on Back Road in Freeport, County of Cumberland, State of Maine, and more fully described in a Deed from Thomas and Marjorie Smith to the Parties dated October 31, 1969 and filed at the Cumberland County Registry of Deeds, Book 4449, Page 34.

IN WITNESS WHEREOF, I have hereunto set my hand and affixed the seal of said District Court this 18 day of November, 19 88.

(SEAL)

____

Title: Clerk, District Court

NAME: Mamie R. Bilideau

This certificate to be recorded in the Registry of Deeds for the county above named.

Return to:

____

____

____

DCCV-20 Rev. (1/86)
CV-39 (1/86)

PART THREE

Special Needs

The following three chapters are for people who have a special problem in connection with their divorce. Chapter 18 deals with the need for court action **before** the divorce is final; Chapter 19 deals with the need for court action to change the judgment **after** the divorce is final; and Chapter 20 describes how to deal with property that wasn't included in the original divorce judgment.

Chapter 18

Motion Pending Divorce

In most divorces, the two spouses can continue to function together until the divorce decree is final. Bills for the family expenses continue to get paid, the children's needs are met, and the couple is able to talk through the various problems which may be a part of day to day living. In short, they are able to basically agree on how to work things out until the divorce.

But, not everyone is able to do this. When one spouse refuses to cooperate in the practical decisions, or refuses to contribute financially to the continued costs of the household or to act in the best interests of your minor children, there is a way to ask the court to make temporary arrangements until the divorce decree is final. This is through the filing of a form, called a Motion Pending Divorce, in the same court which is hearing your divorce.

Even if you and your spouse don't reach agreement right away on various things involved in your divorce, you don't have to file a Motion Pending Divorce. This Motion is used **only** when it is necessary to get a judge involved in order to make sure that you and your children have enough money to live on, that your right to use the family home and property is protected, and that your spouse does not "restrain your personal liberty." (This means that she/he cannot interfere with your life and/or harass you while the divorce is pending in the court). This order remains in effect until the Divorce Decree is final. It can be enforced in court if your spouse does not abide by it.

Because filing such a Motion is a way of recognizing that you can't work things out with your spouse on a temporary basis, most people get lawyers to represent them at this point. You should strongly consider whether you need a lawyer, if you feel that you need an Order Pending Divorce.

However, you can represent yourself on the Motion Pending Divorce if you read this section (and other sections pertaining to child support in Chapter 10, service in Chapter 11, and court testimony in Chapter 15) carefully.

In order to get an Order Pending Divorce, you must first file a "Motion Pending Divorce" form with the District Court which is going to decide your divorce. A sample completed form is provided in this chapter as Form 28. The District Court will probably not have a form that you can purchase for this purpose, so you should type your own using sample Form 28 as a guide. This sample form is written for people who are feeling harrassed, or having other domestic problems. As with all forms, you should only include the specific things which you want the court to do in *your* case.

This Motion Pending Divorce must be served on your spouse in the same way that your Complaint was served. Many people have both the Motion Pending Divorce and the Complaint served at the same time. This isn't necessary, but it may make things easier.

You must also request the court to set a hearing date and time for your Motion. You should tell the Clerk when you think your spouse will be served with the Motion. The hearing will be set at least 7 days **after** your spouse has been served with the Motion. (The notice of when the hearing is scheduled is part of the Motion itself, as Form 28 shows).

If your spouse is not actually served at least 7 days before the hearing, you will have to re-schedule the hearing date.

While most of the language in the Motion contains statements of fact and requests for action by the court, the form includes a reference to the laws which permit this type of motion. It is important to include this language in your Motion. Copies of all sections of the law referred to in this motion are contained in the Appendix, and you should read them over before going to court.

When you file your Motion, you must also include a draft Order Pending Divorce which you would like the Judge to sign in your case. Some courts do sell blank forms which can be used as an Order Pending Divorce. (You should ask the Clerk). Even if your court does not, you can use the blank Order Pending Divorce which is contained in the Appendix by photocopying it and filling in the necessay information. A sample completed Order Pending Divorce is provided in this Chapter as Form 29.

If you or your spouse is receiving, has received, or are likely to be receiving public assistance, you must also notify the Department of Human Services of the date and place of your hearing. Refer to Chapter 6, Section d, for the correct address for the Department of Human Services. You should already have prepared a Certificate of Notice as described in Chapter 10.

At the hearing, you (and any witnesses) will tell the Judge why the temporary Order Pending Divorce is needed. Read Chapter 15 on preparing testimony for the divorce hearing, since the process is very similar. You may also want to observe other hearings on Motions Pending Divorce in your court, in order to become familiar with the process.

If you have children from the marriage, you should complete the Affidavit of Income and Assets and Child Support Worksheet which are available from the court (and explained in Chapter 10, Section j of this book). The court will make a decision about child support on a temporary basis.

One final warning: if your marriage has a history of physical abuse and there is a possibility that your spouse may become violent in reaction to the divorce Complaint, a better option is to get a Protection From Abuse Order from the Court. This process is described in the booklet,*"Protection from Abuse - A Guide to Getting a Court Order Without a Lawyer,"* and it is briefly described in Chapter 8. (This booklet is available from Pine Tree Legal Assistance, police stations, and domestic violence projects around the state). Like a Motion Pending Divorce, the Protection from Abuse Order can include provisions for child custody, support, alimony, and use of the family home. For abused women, a Protection from Abuse Order gives better protection and more legal rights than a Motion Pending Divorce.

FORM 28 -- MOTION AND SUPPORTIVE MEMORANDUM PENDING DIVORCE

STATE OF MAINE

DISTRICT COURT
Division of Eastern Cumberland
Location: Brunswick, Maine
Docket No. ____________________

SUSAN T. BROWN,	*	
Plaintiff	*	MOTION AND SUPPORTIVE MEMORANDUM
-vs-	*	PENDING DIVORCE
JOHN D. BROWN,	*	
Defendant	*	

The Plaintiff Susan T. Brown respectfully requests that the Court make an Order Pending Divorce. In support of this Motion, the Plaintiff states as follows:

1. That she was married to John D. Brown on the 14 day of July, 19 78 in Freeport, ME;

2. That she started a divorce action in this District Court by filing a Complaint for Divorce against John D. Brown, which has been properly served and is now pending;

3. That there are children of this marriage, whose names and dates of birth are as follows: Margaret A. Brown (April 1, 1980); Nathan J. Brown (November 9, 1982); Sally J. Brown (May 5, 1983); Mary P. Brown (October 10, 1988);

4. That the Plaintiff requires that she be permitted to have exclusive possession of the real estate owned by the parties located at Back Road, Freeport, Maine

with household furnishings and furniture pending final disposition of the divorce;

5. That the Defendant is attempting to impose restraint upon the Plaintiff's personal liberty;

6. That the Plaintiff is without means to support herself and the children.

The Plaintiff bases this Motion on 19 M.R.S.A. § 693 and § 752, and Rule 80(c) of the Maine Rules of Civil Procedure.

WHEREFORE, the Plaintiff respectfully requests that, pending the Divorce, the Court will Order the Defendant to pay to said Plaintiff sufficient money for her separate support and for the support of said children in accordance with the child support guidelines.

That the Defendant will be prohibited from imposing any restraint upon the personal liberties of the Plaintiff;

That the Plaintiff may be granted sole parental rights and responsibilities for said children;

That the Plaintiff is to have exclusive possession of their marital home and that the Defendant is ordered to vacate said premises forthwith in accordance;

And that the Court may grant such other and further relief as is appropriate.

Dated at __Freeport__, Maine this __8th__ day of __September__, 19__90__.

By:________________________________
Plaintiff, Pro Se

NOTICE OF MOTION

You are hereby notified that the Plaintiff will request hearing on the within Motion before the ___Eastern Cumberland___ District Court at ___Brunswick___, Maine, on ___September 18th___, 19__90__, at ___9:00 a.m.___, or as soon thereafter as Plaintiff can be heard.

Dated: ___September 8___, 19__90__

____
Plaintiff, Pro Se

FORM 29

ORDER PENDING DIVORCE

STATE OF MAINE

Cumberland County
(Indicate County Where Issued)

District Court
Division of Eastern Cumberland
Location Brunswick, Maine
Docket Number ______

SUSAN T. BROWN *Plaintiff*

vs.

ORDER PENDING DIVORCE

JOHN D. BROWN *Defendant*

HEARING HAD: on the ______ day of ______, 19 ______

It is ORDERED and DECREED that the temporary care and custody of the minor child(ren) Mary P. Brown (October 10, 1987); Margaret A. Brown (April 1, 1980); Nathan J. Brown (November 9, 1982); Sally J. Brown (May 5, 1983) be given to the aforesaid Susan T. Brown until further order of Court, with the right given to the said John D. Brown to visit with said child(ren) and to be visited by said child(ren) at all reasonable times and places.

It is further ORDERED that the aforesaid John D. Brown pay to the aforesaid Susan T. Brown for support of each minor child listed above

the sum of $ 150.00 per week, first payment to be made ______ and each and every week thereafter until further order of Court, payment to be made to the Maine Department of Human Services during such time as Plaintiff/Defendant is receiving state assistance.

It is further ORDERED:

That Susan T. Brown will have exclusive possession of the marital home on Back Road, Freeport, Maine and that John D. Brown will vacate said premises forthwith;

That John D. Brown is prohibited from restraining the personal liberties of Susan T. Brown.

~~It is further ORDERED that the aforesaid ------ pay to ------ for counsel fees incurred in the prosecution of this Petition the sum of ------ dollars.~~

Dated: ______ ______
Judge of District Court

DCCV-15 Rev. (1/83)

Chapter 19

Post-Divorce Motions

a. INTRODUCTION

As we have discussed throughout this manual, there are some parts of your Divorce Judgment that can be changed if your circumstances, or those of your ex-spouse or children change "substantially".

The most common are custody, visitation and child support. Over time, it is likely that someone may want to change the ways these issues were decided in the Divorce Judgment.

Alimony is the only other area which can be changed after the divorce is final by showing that there has been a substantial change in circumstances. A court cannot make any order concerning alimony if there was no alimony ordered in your divorce. YOU CANNOT MODIFY OR CHANGE THE WAY PROPERTY WAS DIVIDED, EVEN IF YOUR CIRCUMSTANCES DO SUBSTANTIALLY CHANGE, (except in very limited cases and they are hard to prove. See Chapter 20).

Frequently, only one person wants to change the Divorce Judgment and the other person opposes that change. For that reason, it is usually necessary to hire a lawyer to represent you.

However, if you and your ex-spouse are in agreement as to how you would like to change the Divorce Judgment, you may be able to represent yourself.

You must bring the action to amend your divorce in the same court where your divorce was granted.

b. WHAT JUSTIFIES A CHANGE IN THE DIVORCE JUDGMENT?

To change a Divorce Judgment, you must show "a substantial change in circumstance" since it was made. With one exception that we discuss below, the law does not say exactly what is meant by "substantial change". The best guidance we can give you is that there must have been **significant** or **important** change since you got the divorce.

For example, if your Divorce Judgment allowed your ex-spouse "reasonable visitation" with your children and you have been unable to agree on what "reasonable" should mean in practical terms (you fight over who gets the children at holidays, vacations, or can't agree on a monthly visitation schedule), this often is enough to have the Divorce Judgment amended.

There are two things which are automatically considered "a substantial change in circumstances" justifying amendment of the Divorce Judgment. The first is where the parents have "shared" or "allocated" parental rights for the children *and* the parent with whom the children are living is thinking about moving out of state. In this type of case, you do not have to convince the court that this is a "substantial change," because the law *says* that it is a substantial change. However, if a parent has "sole" parental rights and responsibilities for the children and that parent is thinking about moving out of state, the other parent can still try to prove that this is a "substantial change". In this case, however, the judge will not automatically consider the move a "substantial change". The parent without custody, opposing the move, will have to prove that it is a "substantial change" justifying an amendment to the Divorce Judgment.

The second is when there is more than a 15% difference between the current amount of child support and the amount which would be ordered under the new child support guidelines. (See Chapter 10(j) to see what support would be ordered under these guidelines).

c. NUTS & BOLTS: AMENDING THE DIVORCE JUDGMENT

If you want to amend a Divorce Judgment, you must follow these steps:

STEP 1 - PREPARE THE PAPERS

You must prepare two legal papers for the court: a "Motion to Amend the Divorce Judgment" and a draft "Amendment to Divorce Judgment".

1. Motion to Amend the Divorce Judgment

The court does not have a form for the "Motion to Amend the Divorce Judgment". A sample completed Motion follows at the end of this chapter as Form 30. Instructions to prepare this form follow.

Refer to the sample completed Form 30 to see where the corresponding letters appear. You will fill in the underlined sections of this form to conform to your own situation. Have a copy of your final Divorce Judgment handy to refer to as you fill out this form.

Instructions on Completing Motion to Amend Divorce Judgment

A through E should be filled in exactly as they appear on your Divorce Judgment.

F. This is the name of the form. Type it exactly as it appears here.

G. If you were the Plaintiff in the divorce, use the word "Plaintiff"; if you were the Defendant, type in "Defendant".

H. Your full name.

I. Depending on what kind of change you want made, complete this section as follows:

For visitation-	"The terms of parent/child contact."
For custody-	"parental rights and responsibilities."
For child support-	"the amount of child support."
For alimony-	"Alimony."

J. Same as G.

K. Fill in the date that the judge signed your Divorce Judgment.

L. Same as I.

M. List your minor children's names and dates of birth on these lines. They should be listed in the same way as on your Divorce Judgment.

N. Fill in here the circumstance that you believe justifies changing the divorce judgment. Some examples follow:

For visitation-	"The children only want to see their father once a month. He refuses to agree to a visitation schedule and blames me for the situation."
For custody-	"The children's father has begun to drink excessively and is abusive to them. They have said they want to live with me."
For child support-	"The children's father has a new job and earns substantially more than he did at the time of the judgment."
For alimony-	"I have become disabled and am unable to work."

O. Repeat the kind of change you want made as stated in I and L above **and** add the specific change you want made. Some examples follow:

For visitation-	"parent/child contact to include a specific visitation schedule."
For custody-	"parental rights and responsibilities to order sole parental rights and responsibilities to the "Plaintiff/Defendant" (use whichever word applies).
For child support-	"child support to require the Plaintiff/Defendant (use whichever word applies) to contribute an amount of support for the child(ren) consistent with his/her (use whichever word applies) present financial circumstances and ability to work."
For alimony-	"alimony to require the Plaintiff/Defendant (use whichever word applies) to contribute an amount of spousal support appropriate under the present circumstances."

P. Add this sentence **only if** you are asking for a change in the amount of child support ordered. Be sure to choose the words that describe the facts of your case. If you are **not** asking for a change in child support, do not include this sentence in your motion at all.

Q. Same as G.

R. Same as K.

S. Same as I.

T. Same as G.

U. Same as G.

V. City or town where you have prepared the Motion.

W. Date you prepared the Motion.

X. Month you prepared the Motion.

Y. Year you prepared the Motion.

Z. **Sign** your full name. Type in either "Plaintiff" or "Defendant", whichever word describes you.

In order to fill in the section of the motion titled "Notice of Hearing", you must contact the court clerk and ask for a date when your motion can be heard. Tell the clerk whether your motion will be contested or uncontested and he/she will set the date accordingly. Once you have the date, you can complete this section.

(If your ex-spouse will contest your motion, you will have to go to mediation — described more fully later. Be sure you have set a date far enough in the future so that you will have completed mediation by the date of the hearing.)

AA. Same as A.

BB. Same as B.

CC. Date for hearing on the motion.

DD. Month of hearing on the motion.

EE. Year of hearing on the motion.

FF. Time of day the motion will be heard.

GG. Type in whether your motion will be heard in the "Morning" or "Afternoon".

HH. Sign your full name. Type in either "Plaintiff" or "Defendant", whichever describes you.

You must prepare a place on the motion for the sheriff to fill out indicating that service has been made on your ex-spouse.

Leave the spaces from (II) and following blank. They will be filled in by the sheriff.

2. Amendment to Divorce Judgment

A form "Amendment to Divorce Judgment" is available from the District Court. A sample completed Amendment appears as Form 31 at the end of this chapter and a blank form is included in the Appendix.

Instructions to complete this form follow. Refer to the sample completed form to see where the corresponding letters appear:

A. - F. Should be filled in exactly as they were on your original Divorce Judgment.

G. Type in the word "Plaintiff" or "Defendant", whichever applies to you **and** your full name.

H. Date of the original Divorce Judgment.

I. The words in the original Divorce Judgment that will be changed by the amendment.

J. The words that you want included in the **new** order made by the judge.

K. - L. Leave these spaces blank. The judge will date and sign the judgment here.

STEP 2 - SERVE THE PAPERS ON ALL NECESSARY PERSONS

You must "serve" a copy of the Motion to Modify your Divorce Decree on your ex-spouse. You must also serve a copy on any other legally concerned people if there are any. For example, if anyone else was given custodial or visitation rights **in your divorce judgment** (such as a grandparent), that person must also be "served" with a copy of the motion.

Your motion must be served **personally** by a sheriff. Refer to the description of how personal service is made in Chapter 11. Remember, you will have to give the sheriff an original and one copy of the motion — one to serve on your ex-spouse and the other, the original, to be returned to you to be filed in court.

Service must be made at least 7 days before the hearing date.

If you are asking that the amount of **child support** be changed **and** your child(ren) have received, are receiving or will receive AFDC, Medicaid or a state SSI supplement check, you **must** notify the Department of Human Services that you are filing a motion to modify your Divorce Judgment. (**You do not have to do this if you are asking for a change in anything other than child support.**) Do this by sending a copy of your motion by regular mail to:

Central Office Supervisor
Division of Support Enforcement
Department of Human Services
State House Station #11
Augusta, Maine 04333

In this case, you must also prepare a "Certificate of Notice" indicating that you have given notice to the Department of Human Services. A sample completed Certificate of Notice appears earlier in this manual as Form 6.

STEP 3 - FILE THE PAPERS IN COURT

You must file the original motion (completed by the sheriff) with the court **promptly** after service has been made. You must also file the "Amendment to Divorce Judgment" that you have prepared at this time. If you are required to file a "Certificate of Notice" you should file this with your motion. Just as in your original divorce, "filing" simply means giving your papers to the court clerk.

At the time that you file your papers, you will be required to pay the court filing fee. If you cannot afford to pay this fee, you can ask the judge to allow you to proceed **In Forma Pauperis,** that is without paying the fee. Chapter 10 describes the procedure for asking the court to allow you to proceed "In Forma Pauperis".

STEP 4 - PREPARE A SETTLEMENT AGREEMENT (If you and your ex-spouse agree.)

If you and your ex-spouse can agree on the proposed amendment, it would be helpful to have a written agreement saying so to give to the judge on the day of the hearing. This is particularly important if your ex-spouse does not plan to go to court with you. Chapter 14 discusses and provides a sample divorce agreement to be used in a divorce action. This form can be modified to use for this purpose.

STEP 5 - PREPARE AN AFFIDAVIT OF INCOME AND ASSETS AND CHILD SUPPORT WORKSHEET (If you want to change the amount of child support.)

These forms must be filled out and brought to mediation (if that has been requested or ordered in your case). If not, they must be filed 3 days before the hearing. Re-read Chapter 10, Section j on how to fill out these forms.

Remember, if the old child support amount varies more than 15% from what would be ordered under the new guidelines, this is a substantial change of circumstance and automatically entitles you to go back to court to change the amount.

STEP 6 - MEDIATION (If you and your ex-spouse don't agree **and** the proposed change involves children.)

If your ex-spouse will **not** agree to the change you want **and** the change involves your child(ren) (e.g., custody, visitation, child support), you will have to go to mediation before you can have a hearing. Reread Chapter 13 describing how to arrange for mediation and what to expect in the process.

STEP 7 - THE DAY OF THE HEARING

a. If your motion is NOT contested.

If you and your ex-spouse are in agreement, you will simply go to court on the day scheduled and ask the judge to make the change requested. You may want to reread Chapter 16 to refresh your memory about court procedures.

Your testimony should simply be a restatement of the facts set out in your motion, including an explanation of the change you want and the "substantial change" in circumstances that you believe justifies it.

The judge will either sign your draft "Amendment to Divorce Judgment" or will have the clerk prepare an order if your draft cannot be used. If you want to know what the judge has decided or you aren't sure you understand the decision, you should ask the judge before you leave the courtroom. Again, the decision will not be final until 10 days after it is entered in the docket by the clerk. During that time either you or your spouse can appeal it. If you aren't satisfied with the decision when you get a copy of it in the mail, you should **immediately** contact a lawyer.

b. If your motion IS contested.

If you and your ex-spouse go through mediation and still cannot agree, you will have to go to a contested hearing. At a contested hearing you and your ex-spouse and other witnesses will have to testify about the things you want changed and the reason why the court should rule for or against you. If it appears that you will have to go to a contested hearing, you are strongly encouraged to get a lawyer to represent you.

FORM 30 -- MOTION AND SUPPORTING MEMORANDUM TO MODIFY DIVORCE JUDGMENT

STATE OF MAINE

DISTRICT COURT
Division of Eastern Cumberland **[A]**
Location: Brunswick, ME ________ **[B]**
Docket No. ____________________ **[C]**

[D] SUSAN T. BROWN,	*	
Plaintiff	*	MOTION AND SUPPORTING MEMORANDUM
-vs-	*	TO MODIFY DIVORCE JUDGMENT **[F]**
[E] JOHN D. BROWN,	*	
Defendant	*	

The Plaintiff [G], ___Susan T. Brown___ **[H]** respectfully requests the Court to amend the Divorce Judgment with respect to the terms of parent/child contact [I]. In support of this motion, the Plaintiff **[J]** states as follows:

1. A Divorce Judgment was granted between the parties on ___October 29, 1988___ **[K]**. The Divorce Judgment set forth in the terms of the divorce, including ___parent/child contact___ **[L]**.

2. There are minor child(ren) of the marriage, namely: Margaret A. Brown (4/1/80); Nathan J. Brown (11/9/82); Sally T. Brown (5/5/83); Mary P. Brown (10/10/88). **[M]**

3. Since then, there has been a substantial change of circumstances in that ___visitation has been unpredictable. The children never know when their father will show up. We need a more certain schedule.___ **[N]**

CONTINUED ON NEXT PAGE

4. Because of this substantial change of circumstances, it is necessary to modify the Divorce Judgment regarding ___________ parent/child contact to including a specific visitation schedule. [O]

(5. The minor children are/are not receiving public assistance while in the custody of the Plaintiff/Defendant.) **[P]**

Modification of the Divorce Judgment under these circumstances is permitted according to 19 M.R.S.A. § 752 and Rule 80(j) of the Maine Rules of Civil Procedure.

WHEREFORE, the Plaintiff **[Q]** respectfully requests that the Court modify the Divorce Judgment signed on October 29, 1988, **[R]** with respect to the terms of parent/child contact. **[S]**

Plaintiff **[T]** further requests that the Court Order the Defendant to reimburse the Plaintiff **[U]** for one half of the costs of mediation, if that becomes necessary, and for such other relief as the Court deems appropriate.

Dated at Freeport **[V]**, Maine this 20th **[W]** day of October **[X]**, 19 90 . **[Y]**

By: Susan T. Brown **[Z]**
Plaintiff/Defendant, Pro Se

CONTINUED ON NEXT PAGE

NOTICE OF HEARING

Please note that this motion will be brought for hearing before the __Eastern Cumberland__**[AA]** District Court, sitting in

__Brunswick__**[BB]** on the __12th__**[CC]** day of __November__**[DD]**,

19_90_**[EE]**, at _9:00__**[FF]** o'clock in the __morning__**[GG]**.

_____Susan T. Brown______**[HH]**
Plaintiff/Defendant, Pro Se

STATE OF MAINE
Cumberland, ss.**[II]**

On the ____________ day of ________________, 19____, I made service of the Motion and Hearing upon __________________________ by delivering a copy thereof to him/her in hand at _______________ ____.

____
Deputy Sheriff

FORM 31

AMENDMENT TO DIVORCE JUDGMENT

STATE OF MAINE

[A] CUMBERLAND County
(Indicate County Where Issued)

District Court
Division of Eastern Cumberland [B]
Location Brunswick, Maine [C]
Docket Number ____________ [D]

E] SUSAN T. BROWN

Plaintiff

vs.

AMENDMENT TO DIVORCE JUDGMENT

F] JOHN D. BROWN

Defendant

HEARING HAD UPON THE MOTION OF THE Plaintiff Susan T. Brown [G] :

It is hereby ORDERED and ADJUDGED that the original Divorce Judgment dated October 29, [H] 1988 be and hereby is altered and ammended by striking out the words:

"The right is given to John D. Brown to have contact with and by said children at all reasonable times." [I]

and inserting in place thereof the words:

John D. Brown will have contact with said children on the first weekend in every month, and will have the children on Christmas Eve and for their birthdays every other year. Additionally, John D. Brown and his only son, Nathan J. Brown, will visit together one additional weekend every month.

in all other respects the original Judgment to remain in full force and effect.

Dated: ____________ [K] ____________ [L]
Judge of District Court

DCCV-18 Rev. (1/83)

Chapter 20

Property Not Included In Your Divorce

If your divorce order left out a specific item (or items) of marital property (as described in Chapter 6), then you may want to file a Motion to "Set Aside Omitted Property" to deal with this problem. By asking the judge to "set aside" omitted property, you are asking that he or she decide who will get property left out of your original divorce judgment.

If you and your ex-spouse are in agreement on who should get the omitted property, you should be able to represent yourself.

However, if the property which was left out of the divorce order is very valuable, and if you cannot agree on how to divide it, then we strongly encourage you to talk with a lawyer about the best way to deal with this situation, in light of the way other property was divided in your divorce.

In order to get an Order to Set Aside Omitted Marital Property, you must first file a "Motion to Set Aside Omitted Marital Property" form with the District Court which decided your divorce. A sample completed form is provided in this chapter as Form 32. The District Court will probably not have a form that you can purchase for this purpose, so you should use this sample Form 32 as a guide.

The "Motion to Set Aside" must be served on your ex-spouse in the same way that your Divorce Complaint was served.

You must also request the Court to set a hearing date and time for your Motion. You should tell the Clerk when you think your ex-spouse will be served with the Motion. The hearing will be set at least 7 days **after** your spouse has been served with the Motion. (The notice of when the hearing is scheduled is part of the Motion itself, as Form 32 shows.)

If your spouse is not actually served at least 7 days before the hearing, you will have to reschedule the hearing date.

There is no court form for this Motion. You will have to type your own using Form 32 as a sample.

We have included two paragraphs in the sample motion which deal with different kinds of property. The first deals with real estate (home, land, etc.) and the second with personal property. Make sure that you include only the kind of property that you want the court to divide in your Motion.

When you file your Motion, you must also include a draft Order for the judge to sign. There is no court form for this either. You will again have to type your own using Form 33 as a sample. As with the Motion, be sure your Order is written to fit your circumstances.

FILL IN THE FORMS

The Caption

Remember to fill in the caption on the Motion exactly the way it appears on your divorce order.

The Motion

[A] Your name

[B] The name of the person who will get the *real* property

[C] The street address, town and county where the property is

[D] The person(s) who sold the property to you and your spouse

[E] The date of the deed to you and your ex-spouse

[F] The county where the property is located

[G] The book number at the Registry of Deeds where the deed appears

[H] The page number at the Registry of Deeds where the deed appears

[I] Your name

[J] Named item of *personal* property

[K] Either your name or that of your ex-spouse, depending on who is to get the property

[L] Your name

[M] The date of your divorce

[N] The date you sign the Motion

[O] Your signature

[P] The District Court where the hearing will be held

[Q] The town where the District Court is located

[R] The day on which the hearing will be held

[S] The month in which the hearing will be held

[T] The time of the hearing

[U] Your signature

[V] The county where service will be made

[W] The day on which the hearing will be held

[X] The month in which the hearing will be held

[Y] Your ex-spouse's name

[Z] The place where your ex-spouse was served

[AA] Do not fill in; this is for the Sheriff's signature

Be sure to fill in the information under the "Notice of Hearing" based on the date and time for the hearing which you have agreed to with the Court Clerk. Remember, it must be actually served on your ex-spouse at least seven days before the date of the hearing.

If real estate was omitted from your divorce decree, you will also need to file a real estate abstract of divorce decree. Follow the directions in Chapter 17, Section b, "Real Estate Abstract of Divorce".

FORM 32 -- MOTION TO SET ASIDE OMITTED MARITAL PROPERTY AND NOTICE OF HEARING

STATE OF MAINE
____________, SS.

DISTRICT COURT
DIV. OF________________
Docket No.______________

______________________	*	
Plaintiff	*	MOTION TO SET ASIDE OMITTED MARITAL PROPERTY AND NOTICE OF HEARING
-vs-	*	
______________________	*	
Defendant	*	

MOTION

Pursuant to 19 M.R.S.A. § 722-A(6), ________[A]________ seeks an order setting aside certain real property to ________[B]__ ____________, consisting of land and buildings located on ________[C]____________________, State of Maine and as more fully described in a Deed from ________[D]__________ to the parties dated ____________[E]________ and filed at the ______[F]______________ County Registry of Deeds, Book ____[G]__ Page __[H]__.

Pursuant to 19 M.R.S.A. § 722-A(6), ________[I]____________ seeks an order setting aside the following items of personal property to the party described below.

______[J]____________ to ________[K]____________

______________________ to ______________________

______________________ to ______________________

In support of this Motion, ____________________[L]__________

states that the above-described property is marital property, and was omitted from the divorce judgment dated __________[M]________.

Dated:________[N]______________ ________________[O]____________________
Plaintiff/Defendant

NOTICE OF HEARING

Please note that this Motion will be brought for hearing before the ______[P]__________________ District Court, sitting in ____________[Q]__________ on the __[R]___ day of __[S]____________, 19___ at _____[T]______ o'clock in the morning/afternoon.

__________[U]_________________________
Plaintiff/Defendant

STATE OF MAINE
_____[V]_________, ss.

On the _____[W]_______ day of _______[X]_____, 1990, I made service of the Motion and Notice upon __________[Y]___________ by delivering a copy thereof to him in hand at ________[Z]________ ___________________________________.

__________[AA]_________________________
Deputy Sheriff

FORM 33 -- ORDER SETTING ASIDE OMITTED MARITAL PROPERTY

STATE OF MAINE

DISTRICT COURT
Division of Eastern Cumberland
Location: Brunswick, ME
Docket No. ________________

SUSAN T. BROWN,	*	
Plaintiff	*	ORDER SETTING ASIDE OMITTED
-vs-	*	MARITAL PROPERTY
JOHN D. BROWN,	*	
Defendant	*	

This matter came before the court on the Motion of Plaintiff Susan T. Brown to set aside certain marital property that was omitted from the parties' Divorce Decree dated October 8, 1988. After hearing, it is **ORDERED** pursuant to 19 M.R.S.A. § 722-A(6) that the omitted marital property be set aside as follows:

1. To Susan T. Brown: Land and buildings located on Back Road in Freeport, County of Cumberland, State of Maine, and more fully described in a Deed from Thomas and Marjorie Smith to the parties dated October 31, 1969 and filed at the Cumberland County Registry of Deeds, Book 4449, Page 34.

Susan T. Brown is responsible for preparing and recording a copy of this decree or an abstract thereof for filing at the Cumberland County Registry of Deeds and for paying all fees necessary therefor.

2. To John D. Brown: An original painting "Dandilyons" by Margaret Van Gogh.

3. The clerk is directed to incorporate this judgment by reference in the docket book.

Date:____________________ ________________________________
Judge, District Court

Appendix

APPENDIX I: LAWS AND RULES

Sections of Laws and Rules

The following sections of Maine Law and Court Rules are what give you the right to court orders pending divorce and post-divorce orders.

The Sections of Law are taken from Title 19 of the Maine Revised Statutes Annotated and the rules from the Maine Rules of Civil Procedure. They are referred to specifically in Forms 28 and 30.

TITLE 19 MAINE REVISED STATUTES ANNOTATED

§ 693. Orders pending divorce

In accordance with section 752, subsection 4, pending a divorce action, the court may order either spouse to pay to the other spouse, or to the attorney for the other spouse, sufficient money for the defense or prosecution thereof; may make reasonable provision for either spouse's separate support, on a motion for which costs and counsel fees may be ordered; enter such decree for the parental rights and responsibilities and support of the minor children, in accordance with Chapter 7, subchapter I-A (the child support guidelines), as the court deems proper; and in all cases enforce obedience by appropriate processes on which costs and counsel fees shall be taxed as in other actions. An order for child support under this section may include an order for the payment of part or all of the medical expenses, hospital expenses and other health care expenses of the children or an order to provide a policy or contract for coverage of those expenses. Availability of public welfare benefits to the family must not affect the decision of the court as to the responsibility of a parent to provide child support.

§ 752. Parenting of children: change of names; compulsory process; support and maintenance

1. Legislative findings and purpose. The Legislature finds and declares as public policy that encouraging mediated resolutions of disputes between parents is in the best interest of minor children.

2. Definitions. As used in this section, unless the context otherwise indicates, the following terms have the following meanings.

A. "Allocated parental rights and responsibilities" means that responsibilities for the various aspects of a child's welfare are divided between the parents, with the parent allocated a particular responsibility having the right to control that aspect of the child's welfare. Responsibilities may be divided exclusively or proportionately. Aspects of a child's welfare for which responsibility may be divided include primary physical residence, parent-child contact, support, education, medical and dental care, religious upbringing, travel boundaries and expenses and any other aspect of parental rights and responsibilities. A parent allocated responsibility for a certain aspect of a child's welfare may be required to inform the other parent of major changes in that aspect.

B. "Child support" means money to be paid directly to a parent, to another person or agency awarded parental rights and responsibilities with respect to a child, or to the Department of Human Services on behalf of any child receiving public assistance and any medical or dental insurance coverage provided to a child pursuant to court order.

C. "Shared parental rights and responsibilities" means that most or all aspects of a child's welfare remain the joint responsibility and right of both parents, so that both parents retain equal parental rights and responsibilities and both parents must confer and make joint decisions regarding the child's welfare.

D. "Sole parental rights and responsibilities" means that one parent is granted exclusive parental rights and responsibilities with respect to all aspects of a child's welfare, with the possible exception of the right and responsibility for support.

3. Jurisdiction. The court making an order of nullity or of divorce may make an order awarding parental rights and responsibilities with respect to a minor child of the parties.

4. Mediation. Prior to a contested hearing under this section where there are minor children of the parties, the court shall refer the parties to mediation; except that, for good cause shown, the court, prior to referring the parties to mediation, may hear motions for temporary relief, pending final judgment on any issue or combination of issues for which good cause for temporary relief has been shown. Upon motion supported by affidavit, the court may, for extraordinary cause shown, waive the mediation requirement under this subsection. Any agreement reached by the parties through mediation on any issues shall be reduced to writing, signed by the parties and presented to the court for approval as a court order. When agreement through mediation is not reached on any issue, the court must determine that the parties made a good faith effort to mediate the issue before proceeding with a hearing. If the court finds that either party failed to make a good faith effort to mediate, the court may order the parties to submit to mediation, may dismiss the action or any part of the action, may render a decision or judgment by default, may assess attorney's fees and costs or may impose any other sanction that is appropriate in the circumstances. The court may also impose an appropriate sanction upon a party's failure without good cause to appear for mediation after receiving notice of the scheduled time for mediation.

5. Best interest of the child. The court, in making an award of parental rights and responsibilities with respect to a minor child, shall apply the standard of the best interest of the child. In applying this standard, the court shall consider the following factors:

A. The age of the child;
B. The relationship of the child with the child's parents and any other persons who may significantly affect the child's welfare;
C. The preference of the child, if old enough to express a meaningful preference;
D. The duration and adequacy of the child's current living arrangements and the desirability of maintaining continuity;
E. The stability of any proposed living arrangements for the child;
F. The motivation of the parties involved and their capacities to give the child love, affection and guidance;
G. The child's adjustment to the child's present home, school and community;
H. The capacity of each parent to allow and encourage frequent and continuing contact between the child and the other parent, including physical access;
I. The capacity of each parent to cooperate or to learn to cooperate in child care;
J. Methods for assisting parental cooperation and resolving disputes and each parent's willingness to use those methods;
K. The effect on the child if one parent has sole authority over the child's upbringing; and
L. All other factors having a reasonable bearing on the physical and psychological well-being of the child.

6. Order. The order of the court shall award allocated parental rights and responsibilities, shared parental rights and responsibilities or sole parental rights and responsibilities, according to the best interest of the child. Where the parents have agreed to an award of shared parental rights and responsibilities or so agree in open court, the court shall make that award unless there is substantial evidence that it should not be ordered. The court shall state in its decision the reasons for not ordering a shared parental rights and responsibilities award agreed to by the parents.

The court may award reasonable rights of contact with a minor child to any 3rd persons.

The court may award parental rights and responsibilities with respect to the child to a 3rd person, some suitable society or institution for the care and protection of children or the Department of Human Services upon a finding that awarding parental rights and responsibilities to either or both parents will place the child in jeopardy as defined in Title 22, section 4002, subsection 6.

Every final order issued under this section shall contain

A. A provision for child support or a statement of the reasons for not ordering child support; and

B. A statement that each parent shall have access to records and information pertaining to a minor child, including but not limited to, medical, dental and school records, whether or not the child resides with the parent, unless that access is found not to be in the best interest of the child or that access is found to be sought for the purpose of causing detriment to the other parent. If that access is not ordered, the court shall state in the order its reasons for denying that access.

7. Equal consideration of parents. The court may not apply a preference for one parent over the other in determining parental rights and responsibilities because of the parent's sex or the child's age or sex.

8. Abandonment of family residence. The court shall not consider abandonment of the family residence as a factor in determining parental rights and responsibilities with respect to a minor child when the abandoning parent has been physically harmed or seriously threatened with physical harm by the other parent and that harm or threat of harm was causally related to the abandonment, or when one parent has left the family residence at the request or insistence of the other parent.

9. Departmentof Human Services. When the Department of Human Services has been granted parental rights and responsibilities for a child under this section, Title 22, chapter 1071, shall apply regarding subsequent reviews and shall govern further rights and responsibilities of the department, the parents, the child and any other party.

10. Support order. An order of the court for child support may run against the father or the mother in whole or in part or against both, irrespective of the fault of the father or mother in the divorce action. For divorces ordered after January 1, 1990, the order for child support may run until the child graduates, withdraws or is expelled from secondary school as defined in Title 20-A, section 1, or attains the age of 19 years, whichever first occurs after the child attains the age of 18 years. When the order is to run against both, the court shall specify the amount each shall pay. The court shall inquire of the parties concerning the existence of a child support order entered pursuant to chapter 7, subchapter V. If such an order exists, the court shall consider its terms in establishing a child support obligation. A determination or modification of child support under this section must comply with chapter 7, subchapter I-A.

An order for child support under this section may include an order for the payment of part or all of the medical expenses, hospital expenses and other health care expenses of the child. The court order must include a provision requiring an obligated parent to obtain and maintain health insurance coverage for medical, hospitalization and dental expenses, if health insurance is available to the obligated parent at reasonable cost. The court order must also require the obligated parent to furnish proof of such coverage to the obligee within 15 days of receipt of a copy of the court order. For the purposes of this section, health insurance is considered reasonable in cost if it is employment-related or other group health insurance. If health insurance is not available at reasonable cost at the time of the hearing, the court order must establish the obligation to provide health insurance on the part of the obligated parent effective immediately upon the insurance being available at reasonable cost.

Availability of public welfare benefits to the family shall not affect the decision of the court as to the responsibility of a parent to provide child support.
The court may enforce a support order as provided in chapter 14A.

11. **Name change.** Upon the request of the wife during the action for divorce or annulment or at any time thereafter, the court may change the name of the wife.

12. **Modification of orders; compulsory process.** Upon the motion of one or both of the parents; or any agency or person who has been granted parental rights and responsibilities or contact with respect to a child under this section, the court may alter its order concerning parental rights and responsibilities or contact with respect to a minor child as circumstances require. Child support orders may be modified retroactively, but only from the date that notice of a petition for modification has been served upon the opposing party pursuant to the Maine Rules of Civil Procedure. The parties shall be referred to mediation as under subsection 4.

The relocation, or intended relocation, of a child resident in this State to another state by a parent, when the other parent is a resident in this State and there exists an award of shared or allocated parental rights and responsibilities concerning the child, is a substantial change in circumstances.

In execution of the powers given it under this Title, the court may employ any compulsory process which it deems proper, by execution, attachment or other effectual form, on which costs shall be taxed as in other actions.

13. **Uniform Child Custody Jurisdiction Act.** The jurisdiction granted by this section to make or alter an order concerning parental rights and responsibilities with respect to a minor child shall be limited by the Uniform Child Custody Jurisdiction Act, sections 801 to 825, if another state may have jurisdiction as provided in that Act.

Rule 80 (c) Orders Prior to Judgment. At any time prior to judgment in any action under this rule in which the court has personal jurisdiction over the parties, the court may on motion after notice served not later than 7 days before the hearing, order either party to pay the other party or to that party's attorney sufficient money for the defense or prosecution thereof, and to make reasonable provision for that party's separate support, and may make such orders as it deems proper for the care, custody and support of minor children. At any time prior to judgment in any action under this rule the court may on motion after notice served not later than 7 days before the hearing, enter such order as it deems proper for the custody of minor children subject to the jurisdiction of the court and may prohibit either party from imposing any restraint on the personal liberty of the other. Costs may be taxed and counsel fees may be ordered on any motion under this subdivision and the court may in all cases enforce obedience as in other actions. Execution for counsel fees shall not issue until after entry of final judgment. Rules 7(c) and (e) shall not apply to motions brought pursuant to this subdivision.

Rule 80 (j) Manner of Service on Divorce Motions. Any proceedings for modification or enforcement of the judgment in an action for divorce shall be on motion, a copy of which together with notice of hearing as provided in Rule 7(b)(3) shall be served in accordance with Rule 4, except that service within the state shall be by delivery to the party personally unless otherwise ordered by the court; provided that, when a motion is made in response to a motion filed by a party represented by an attorney, the responsive motion may be served upon the attorney in accordance with Rule 5(b) of these rules.

CHILD SUPPORT TABLE

SCHEDULE OF BASIC WEEKLY CHILD SUPPORT ENTITLEMENTS
(PER CHILD, PER WEEK, ROUNDED TO THE NEAREST DOLLAR)

Ages of Children: Age 0 thru 11 Years

Parents' Combined Annual Gross Income	Number of Children 1	2	3	4	5	6
$6,000	16	9	6	4	4	3
$6,600	22	12	8	6	5	4
$7,200	26	15	10	8	7	5
$7,800	28	18	13	10	8	7
$8,400	30	21	15	12	9	8
$9,000	32	24	17	13	11	9
$9,600	33	26	20	15	12	10
$10,200	35	27	22	17	14	11
$10,800	36	28	24	18	15	12
$11,400	38	30	25	20	16	14
$12,000	40	31	26	22	17	15
$12,600	41	32	27	22	19	16
$13,200	43	33	28	23	20	17
$13,800	44	34	29	24	21	18
$14,400	46	35	30	25	22	19
$15,000	47	37	31	26	23	20
$15,600	48	38	31	27	23	21
$16,200	50	39	32	27	24	21
$16,800	51	40	33	28	24	22
$17,400	52	40	34	29	25	22
$18,000	53	41	35	29	25	23
$18,600	54	42	35	30	26	23
$19,200	56	43	36	31	27	24
$19,800	57	44	37	31	27	24
$20,400	58	45	38	32	28	25
$21,000	59	46	38	32	28	25
$21,600	60	47	39	33	29	26
$22,200	62	48	40	34	29	26
$22,800	63	49	41	34	30	27
$23,400	64	50	41	35	31	27
$24,000	65	51	42	36	31	28
$24,600	66	51	43	36	32	28
$25,200	67	52	44	37	32	29
$25,800	69	53	44	38	33	29
$26,400	70	54	45	38	33	30
$27,000	71	55	46	39	34	30
$27,600	72	56	47	39	34	31
$28,200	73	57	47	40	35	31
$28,800	74	58	48	41	36	32
$29,400	76	58	49	41	36	32
$30,000	77	59	50	42	37	33

Ages of Children: Age 12 thru 17 Years

Parents' Combined Annual Gross Income	Number of Children 1	2	3	4	5	6
$6,000	17	9	6	5	4	3
$6,600	23	12	8	6	5	4
$7,200	30	16	11	8	7	6
$7,800	35	19	13	10	8	7
$8,400	37	23	15	12	9	8
$9,000	39	26	18	13	11	9
$9,600	41	30	20	15	12	10
$10,200	43	33	22	17	14	11
$10,800	45	35	24	19	15	13
$11,400	47	37	27	20	16	14
$12,000	49	38	29	22	18	15
$12,600	51	39	31	23	19	16
$13,200	53	41	33	25	20	17
$13,800	54	42	35	27	22	18
$14,400	56	44	37	28	23	19
$15,000	58	45	38	30	24	20
$15,600	60	47	39	32	25	21
$16,200	61	48	40	33	27	22
$16,800	63	49	41	35	28	23
$17,400	64	50	42	35	29	24
$18,000	66	51	43	36	30	25
$18,600	67	52	44	37	31	26
$19,200	69	53	45	38	33	27
$19,800	70	55	46	39	34	28
$20,400	72	56	46	39	34	29
$21,000	73	57	47	40	35	30
$21,600	75	58	48	41	36	31
$22,200	76	59	49	42	36	32
$22,800	78	60	50	43	37	33
$23,400	79	61	51	43	38	34
$24,000	80	63	52	44	39	34
$24,600	82	64	53	45	39	35
$25,200	83	65	54	46	40	35
$25,800	85	66	55	46	40	36
$26,400	86	67	56	47	41	37
$27,000	87	68	57	48	42	37
$27,600	89	69	58	49	42	38
$28,200	90	70	58	49	43	38
$28,800	92	71	59	50	44	39
$29,400	93	72	60	51	45	40
$30,000	95	74	61	52	45	40

SCHEDULE OF BASIC WEEKLY CHILD SUPPORT ENTITLEMENTS
(PER CHILD, PER WEEK, ROUNDED TO THE NEAREST DOLLAR)

Parents' Combined Annual Gross Income	Ages of Children: Age 0 thru 11 Years — Number of Children: 1	2	3	4	5	6	Parents' Combined Annual Gross Income	Ages of Children: Age 12 thru 17 Years — Number of Children: 1	2	3	4	5	6
$30,600	78	60	50	43	37	33	$30,600	96	75	62	53	46	41
$31,200	79	61	51	43	38	34	$31,200	97	76	63	53	47	41
$31,800	80	62	52	44	38	34	$31,800	99	77	64	54	47	42
$32,400	81	63	52	44	39	34	$32,400	100	78	65	55	48	43
$33,000	82	64	53	45	39	35	$33,000	101	79	66	56	48	43
$33,600	83	64	54	46	40	35	$33,600	103	80	67	56	49	44
$34,200	84	65	55	46	40	36	$34,200	104	81	67	57	50	44
$34,800	85	66	55	47	41	36	$34,800	105	82	68	58	50	45
$35,400	87	67	56	47	41	37	$35,400	107	83	69	58	51	46
$36,000	88	68	57	48	42	37	$36,000	108	84	70	59	52	46
$36,600	89	69	57	48	42	38	$36,600	109	85	71	60	52	47
$37,200	90	69	58	49	43	38	$37,200	111	86	72	61	53	47
$37,800	91	70	59	50	43	39	$37,800	112	87	72	61	53	48
$38,400	92	71	59	50	44	39	$38,400	113	88	73	62	54	48
$39,000	93	72	60	51	44	39	$39,000	114	89	74	63	55	49
$39,600	94	73	61	51	45	40	$39,600	116	90	75	63	55	49
$40,200	95	73	61	52	45	40	$40,200	117	91	76	64	56	50
$40,800	96	74	62	52	46	41	$40,800	118	92	77	65	56	50
$41,400	97	75	63	53	46	41	$41,400	119	93	77	65	57	51
$42,000	98	76	63	53	47	42	$42,000	121	94	78	66	58	51
$42,600	99	77	64	54	47	42	$42,600	122	95	79	67	58	52
$43,200	100	77	65	55	48	42	$43,200	123	96	80	68	59	53
$43,800	101	78	65	55	48	43	$43,800	125	97	81	68	60	53
$44,400	102	79	66	56	49	43	$44,400	126	98	82	69	60	54
$45,000	103	80	67	56	49	44	$45,000	127	99	82	70	61	54
$45,600	104	81	67	57	50	44	$45,600	129	100	83	70	61	55
$46,200	105	82	68	58	50	45	$46,200	130	101	84	71	62	55
$46,800	106	83	69	58	51	45	$46,800	131	102	85	72	63	56
$47,400	107	83	70	59	51	46	$47,400	133	103	86	73	63	57
$48,000	109	84	70	59	52	46	$48,000	134	104	87	73	64	57
$48,600	110	85	71	60	52	47	$48,600	135	105	88	74	65	58
$49,200	111	86	72	61	53	47	$49,200	137	106	89	75	65	58
$49,800	112	87	72	61	53	48	$49,800	138	107	89	76	66	59
$50,400	113	88	73	62	54	48	$50,400	139	108	90	76	67	59
$51,000	114	88	74	62	54	48	$51,000	141	109	91	77	67	60
$51,600	115	89	74	63	55	49	$51,600	142	110	92	78	68	61
$52,200	116	90	75	64	55	49	$52,200	143	111	93	79	69	61
$52,800	117	91	76	64	56	50	$52,800	145	112	94	79	69	62
$53,400	118	92	77	65	56	50	$53,400	146	113	95	80	70	62
$54,000	119	93	77	65	57	51	$54,000	147	114	96	81	70	63

SCHEDULE OF BASIC WEEKLY CHILD SUPPORT ENTITLEMENTS
(PER CHILD, PER WEEK, ROUNDED TO THE NEAREST DOLLAR)

Parents' Combined Annual Gross Income	Ages of Children: Age 0 thru 11 Years — Number of Children: 1	2	3	4	5	6	Parents' Combined Annual Gross Income	Ages of Children: Age 12 thru 17 Years — Number of Children: 1	2	3	4	5	6
$54,600	120	94	78	66	58	51	$54,600	149	115	96	81	71	63
$55,200	121	94	79	66	58	52	$55,200	150	116	97	82	72	64
$55,800	123	95	79	67	59	52	$55,800	151	118	98	83	72	65
$56,400	124	96	80	68	59	53	$56,400	153	119	99	84	73	65
$57,000	125	97	81	68	60	53	$57,000	154	120	100	84	74	66
$57,600	126	98	81	69	60	54	$57,600	155	121	101	85	74	66
$58,200	127	99	82	69	61	54	$58,200	157	122	102	86	75	67
$58,800	128	99	83	70	61	54	$58,800	158	123	103	87	76	67
$59,400	129	100	84	71	62	55	$59,400	159	124	103	87	76	68
$60,000	130	101	84	71	62	55	$60,000	161	125	104	88	77	68
$60,600	131	102	85	72	63	56	$60,600	162	125	105	89	77	69
$61,200	132	102	85	72	63	56	$61,200	163	126	106	89	78	69
$61,800	133	103	86	73	63	57	$61,800	164	127	106	90	78	70
$62,400	134	104	87	73	64	57	$62,400	165	128	107	91	79	70
$63,000	135	105	87	74	64	57	$63,000	167	129	108	91	80	71
$63,600	136	105	88	74	65	58	$63,600	168	130	109	92	80	71
$64,200	137	106	89	75	65	58	$64,200	169	131	110	93	81	72
$64,800	138	107	89	75	66	59	$64,800	170	132	110	93	81	73
$65,400	139	108	90	76	66	59	$65,400	171	133	111	94	82	73
$66,000	140	109	91	77	67	60	$66,000	173	134	112	95	83	74
$66,600	141	109	91	77	67	60	$66,600	174	135	113	95	83	74
$67,200	142	110	92	78	68	60	$67,200	175	136	114	96	84	75
$67,800	143	111	92	78	68	61	$67,800	176	137	114	97	84	75
$68,400	144	112	93	79	69	61	$68,400	177	138	115	97	85	76
$69,000	145	112	94	79	69	62	$69,000	179	139	116	98	85	76
$69,600	146	113	94	80	70	62	$69,600	180	140	117	99	86	77
$70,200	147	114	95	80	70	62	$70,200	181	141	117	99	87	77
$70,800	148	115	96	81	71	63	$70,800	182	142	118	100	87	78
$71,400	148	115	96	81	71	63	$71,400	184	142	119	101	88	78
$72,000	149	116	97	82	71	64	$72,000	185	143	120	101	88	79
$72,600	150	117	98	82	72	64	$72,600	186	144	121	102	89	79
$73,200	151	118	98	83	72	65	$73,200	187	145	121	103	90	80
$73,800	152	118	99	84	73	65	$73,800	188	146	122	103	90	80
$74,400	153	119	99	84	73	65	$74,400	190	147	123	104	91	81
$75,000	154	120	100	85	74	66	$75,000	191	148	124	105	91	81
$75,600	155	121	101	85	74	66	$75,600	192	149	124	105	92	82
$76,200	156	121	101	86	75	67	$76,200	193	150	125	106	92	82
$76,800	157	122	102	86	75	67	$76,800	194	151	126	107	93	83
$77,400	158	123	103	87	76	68	$77,400	196	152	127	107	94	83
$78,000	159	124	103	87	76	68	$78,000	197	153	128	108	94	84

SCHEDULE OF BASIC WEEKLY CHILD SUPPORT ENTITLEMENTS
(PER CHILD, PER WEEK, ROUNDED TO THE NEAREST DOLLAR)

Parents' Combined Annual Gross Income	Ages of Children: Age 0 thru 11 Years — Number of Children 1	2	3	4	5	6	Parents' Combined Annual Gross Income	Ages of Children: Age 12 thru 17 Years — Number of Children 1	2	3	4	5	6
$78,600	160	125	104	88	77	68	$78,600	198	154	128	109	95	84
$79,200	161	125	105	88	77	69	$79,200	199	155	129	109	95	85
$79,800	162	126	105	89	78	69	$79,800	201	156	130	110	96	85
$80,400	163	127	106	89	78	70	$80,400	202	157	131	111	97	86
$81,000	164	128	106	90	79	70	$81,000	203	158	132	111	97	86
$81,600	165	128	107	90	79	70	$81,600	204	158	132	112	98	87
$82,200	166	129	107	91	79	71	$82,200	205	159	133	112	98	87
$82,800	166	129	108	91	80	71	$82,800	206	160	133	113	98	88
$83,400	167	130	108	92	80	71	$83,400	207	160	134	113	99	88
$84,000	168	130	109	92	80	72	$84,000	208	161	134	114	99	88
$84,600	169	131	109	92	81	72	$84,600	209	162	135	114	100	89
$85,200	169	131	110	93	81	72	$85,200	209	162	136	115	100	89
$85,800	170	132	110	93	81	72	$85,800	210	163	136	115	100	90
$86,400	171	133	111	94	82	73	$86,400	211	164	137	116	101	90
$87,000	171	133	111	94	82	73	$87,000	212	164	137	116	101	90
$87,600	172	134	112	94	82	73	$87,600	213	165	138	116	102	91
$88,200	173	134	112	95	83	74	$88,200	214	166	138	117	102	91
$88,800	174	135	112	95	83	74	$88,800	215	166	139	117	103	91
$89,400	174	135	113	96	83	74	$89,400	216	167	140	118	103	92
$90,000	175	136	113	96	84	75	$90,000	217	168	140	118	103	92
$90,600	176	136	114	96	84	75	$90,600	218	169	141	119	104	93
$91,200	177	137	114	97	84	75	$91,200	219	169	141	119	104	93
$91,800	177	138	115	97	85	75	$91,800	220	170	142	120	105	93
$92,400	178	138	115	97	85	76	$92,400	220	171	142	120	105	94
$93,000	179	139	116	98	85	76	$93,000	221	171	143	121	106	94
$93,600	179	139	116	98	86	76	$93,600	222	172	144	121	106	94
$94,200	180	140	116	99	86	77	$94,200	223	173	144	122	106	95
$94,800	181	140	117	99	86	77	$94,800	224	173	145	122	107	95
$95,400	182	141	117	99	87	77	$95,400	225	174	145	123	107	96
$96,000	182	141	118	100	87	78	$96,000	226	175	146	123	108	96
$96,600	183	142	118	100	87	78	$96,600	227	175	146	124	108	96
$97,200	184	143	119	100	88	78	$97,200	227	176	147	124	108	97
$97,800	184	143	119	101	88	78	$97,800	228	176	147	124	109	97
$98,400	185	143	119	101	88	79	$98,400	229	177	148	125	109	97
$99,000	185	144	120	101	89	79	$99,000	230	178	148	125	109	97
$99,600	186	144	120	102	89	79	$99,600	230	178	149	126	110	98
$100,200	186	145	121	102	89	79	$100,200	231	179	149	126	110	98
$100,800	187	145	121	102	89	80	$100,800	232	179	150	126	110	98
$101,400	188	146	121	103	90	80	$101,400	232	180	150	127	111	99
$102,000	188	146	122	103	90	80	$102,000	233	180	151	127	111	99

SCHEDULE OF BASIC WEEKLY CHILD SUPPORT ENTITLEMENTS
(PER CHILD, PER WEEK, ROUNDED TO THE NEAREST DOLLAR)

Parents' Combined Annual Gross Income	Ages of Children: Age 0 thru 11 Years — Number of Children: 1	2	3	4	5	6	Parents' Combined Annual Gross Income	Ages of Children: Age 12 thru 17 Years — Number of Children: 1	2	3	4	5	6
$102,600	189	147	122	103	90	80	$102,600	234	181	151	128	111	99
$103,200	189	147	123	104	90	81	$103,200	234	181	152	128	112	100
$103,800	190	148	123	104	91	81	$103,800	235	182	152	128	112	100
$104,400	190	148	123	104	91	81	$104,400	236	183	153	129	112	100
$105,000	191	149	124	105	91	81	$105,000	236	183	153	129	113	101
$105,600	191	149	124	105	92	82	$105,600	237	184	154	130	113	101
$106,200	192	150	125	105	92	82	$106,200	238	184	154	130	113	101
$106,800	193	150	125	106	92	82	$106,800	238	185	155	130	114	101
$107,400	193	151	125	106	92	82	$107,400	239	185	155	131	114	102
$108,000	194	151	126	106	93	83	$108,000	240	186	156	131	115	102
$108,600	194	152	126	106	93	83	$108,600	240	187	156	131	115	102
$109,200	195	152	127	107	93	83	$109,200	241	187	157	132	115	103
$109,800	195	153	127	107	94	83	$109,800	242	188	157	132	116	103
$110,400	196	153	127	107	94	84	$110,400	242	188	157	133	116	103
$111,000	196	154	128	108	94	84	$111,000	243	189	158	133	116	104
$111,600	197	154	128	108	94	84	$111,600	244	189	158	133	117	104
$112,200	197	154	128	108	95	84	$112,200	244	190	159	134	117	104
$112,800	198	155	129	109	95	85	$112,800	245	190	159	134	117	104
$113,400	198	155	129	109	95	85	$113,400	245	191	159	134	117	105
$114,000	199	155	129	109	95	85	$114,000	246	191	160	135	118	105
$114,600	199	156	130	109	95	85	$114,600	246	191	160	135	118	105
$115,200	200	156	130	110	96	85	$115,200	247	192	161	135	118	105
$115,800	200	156	130	110	96	85	$115,800	247	192	161	136	118	106
$116,400	201	157	130	110	96	86	$116,400	248	193	161	136	119	106
$117,000	201	157	131	110	96	86	$117,000	248	193	162	136	119	106
$117,600	201	157	131	110	96	86	$117,600	249	193	162	136	119	106
$118,200	202	158	131	111	97	86	$118,200	250	194	162	137	119	106
$118,800	202	158	132	111	97	86	$118,800	250	194	163	137	120	107
$119,400	203	158	132	111	97	87	$119,400	251	195	163	137	120	107
$120,000	203	159	132	111	97	87	$120,000	251	195	163	138	120	107
$120,600	204	159	132	112	97	87	$120,600	252	196	164	138	120	107
$121,200	204	159	133	112	98	87	$121,200	252	196	164	138	121	108
$121,800	205	160	133	112	98	87	$121,800	253	196	164	139	121	108
$122,400	205	160	133	112	98	88	$122,400	253	197	165	139	121	108
$123,000	205	160	134	113	98	88	$123,000	254	197	165	139	121	108
$123,600	206	161	134	113	99	88	$123,600	254	198	165	139	122	109
$124,200	206	161	134	113	99	88	$124,200	255	198	166	140	122	109
$124,800	207	161	134	113	99	88	$124,800	255	198	166	140	122	109
$125,400	207	162	135	114	99	88	$125,400	256	199	167	140	122	109
$126,000	208	162	135	114	99	89	$126,000	257	199	167	141	123	109
$126,600	208	162	135	114	100	89	$126,600	257	200	167	141	123	110

Criteria For Deviating From Support Guidelines

These are reasons that a judge may use to order a child support amount different from the amount of the child support table.

A. The non-primary residential care provider is in fact providing primary residential care for more than 30% of the time on an annual basis;

B. The number of children for whom support is being determined is greater than six (6);

C. The interrelation of the total support obligation established under the support guidelines for child support, the division of property and any award of spousal support made in the same proceeding for which a parental support obligation is being determined;

D. The financial resources of the child or children;

E. The financial resources and needs of a party, including non-recurring income not included in the definition of gross income;

F. The standard of living the child or children would have enjoyed had the marital relationship continued;

G. The physical and emotional conditions of the child or children;

H. The educational needs of the child or children;

I. Inflation with relation to the cost of living;

J. Available income and financial contributions of the domestic associate or current spouse of each party;

K. The existence of other persons who are actually financially dependent on either party, including, but not limited to, elderly, disabled or infirm relatives, or adult children pursuing post-secondary education. If the primary care provider is legally responsible for other minor children who reside in the household and if the computation of a theoretical support obligation on behalf of the primary care provider would result in a significantly greater parental support obligation on the part of the non-primary care provider, that factor may be considered;

L. The tax consequences of a support award, including the substantial monetary benefit that a party may derive from any federal tax credit for child care expenses;

M. The fact that the incremental cost of health insurance premiums required to be paid by a party, notwithstanding the deduction of these premiums from gross income, exceeds 15% of that party's share of the total support obligation;

N. The fact that income at a reasonable rate of return may be imputed to non-income-producing assets with an aggregate fair market value of $10,000 or more, other than an ordinary residence or other asset from which the children derive a substantial benefit;

O. The existence of special circumstances regarding a child 12 years of age or over that for the child's best interest requires that the primary residential care provider continue to provide for employment-related day care;

P. An obligor party's substantial financial obligation regarding the costs of transportation of the child or children for purposes of parent and child contact. To be considered substantial, the transportation costs must exceed 15% of the yearly support obligation; and

Q. A finding by the court or hearing officer that the application of the support guidelines would be unjust, inappropriate or not in the child's best interest.

APPENDIX III: COURT FORMS

STATE OF MAINE

District Court
Division of ____________________________
Location ______________________________
Docket No. _____________________________

______________________________ Plaintiff

vs.

COMPLAINT FOR DIVORCE

______________________________ Defendant

1. Plaintiff was lawfully married to ____
at ___________________________________ in the County of ____________________
and State of ________________ on the ______________ day of ______________, 19______.

2. Plaintiff resides in [town or city]____________________________, [State]__________________.

3. (Defendant resides in [town or city]____________________________, [State]__________________.)
(The residence of Defendant is unknown to Plaintiff and cannot be ascertained by reasonable diligence.)
[Delete statement that does not apply. If residence of Defendant is unknown, complete the affidavit on the reverse side.]

4. This court has jurisdiction because (check the following statements that are applicable):
[ ] A. Plaintiff has resided in this State in good faith for six months prior to the commencement of this action;
[ ] B. Plaintiff is a resident of this State and the parties were married in this State;
[ ] C. Plaintiff is a resident of this State and the parties resided in this State when the cause of action accrued;
[ ] D. Defendant is a resident of this State;

5. The only other divorce or annulment actions previously commenced between the parties, together with the designation of the court or courts involved and the disposition thereof, are as follows:
____
____

6. There is real and personal property of the parties as defined by 19 M.R.S.A. § 722-A, as amended;

7. Plaintiff asserts the following grounds for divorce (check the applicable ground):
[ ] A. Irreconcilable marital differences exist between the parties;
[ ] B. Defendant has been guilty of cruel and abusive treatment towards Plaintiff;
[ ] C. Other ____.

8. The following child(ren) have been born to the parties (list children including date of birth):
____
____
An affidavit concerning child custody is attached hereto. *Check one of the following:*
[ ] A. (Plaintiff) (Defendant) is receiving, has received or will be receiving public assistance for the above child(ren).
[ ] B. No one is receiving, has received or will be receiving public assistance for the above child(ren).

9. There is no collusion between Plaintiff and Defendant to obtain a divorce.

DCCV 14 Rev. (11/86)

WHEREFORE, Plaintiff prays that a divorce from the bonds of matrimony between Plaintiff and Defendant be adjudged;

That the parental rights and responsibilities regarding the minor child(ren), including child support payments, be determined;

That the Court set apart to each party his or her property and divide the marital property pursuant to Title 19, M.R.S.A. § 722-A;

That reasonable alimony, or a specific sum in lieu thereof, be ordered paid to Plaintiff by Defendant;

That reasonable counsel fees be ordered paid by Defendant to ______________________________ Attorney for Plaintiff, execution to issue therefor when decree of divorce is granted; and

That Plaintiff be allowed to change her name to ______________________________.

Dated at ______________________, Maine, this______ day of ______________, 19____.

By:______________________________ ______________________________
(Attorney for) Plaintiff Plaintiff

____
Address

____

____
Telephone

****

STATE OF MAINE

______________________ County

Personally appeared ______________________________ above named Plaintiff and made Oath that the foregoing allegation as to the residence of the Defendant is true.

Before me,

____
Notary Public / Attorney at Law

STATE OF MAINE

(Seal of the Court)

District Court Seven
Division of Southern Kennebec
Location Augusta, Maine
Docket No. ____________

____________ Plaintiff

DIVORCE SUMMONS

vs.

____________ Defendant

To the Defendant ____________
Address: ____________
____

The Plaintiff ____________ has begun a lawsuit against you in the District Court which holds sessions at ____________ in ____________ County. If you wish to oppose the divorce, you or your attorney MUST FILE A WRITTEN ANSWER to the attached Complaint within 20 days from the day this Summons was served upon you. You or your attorney must file your Answer by delivering it in person or by mail to the office of the Clerk of the District Court, ____________ Street, ____________ Maine. On or before the day you file your Answer, you or your attorney must mail a copy of your Answer to the (Attorney for) Plaintiff, whose address appears below.

IMPORTANT WARNING: IF YOU FAIL TO FILE AN ANSWER WITHIN THE TIME STATED ABOVE, OR IF YOU FAIL TO APPEAR AT ANY TIME THE COURT NOTIFIES YOU TO DO SO, A JUDGMENT BY DEFAULT MAY BE ENTERED AGAINST YOU IN YOUR ABSENCE FOR THE DIVORCE AND ANY OTHER RELIEF DEMANDED.

IF YOU DO NOT FILE AN ANSWER, BUT YOU WISH TO BE ADVISED OF THE DATE OF HEARING OR TO BE HEARD ON PARENTAL RIGHTS OF CHILDREN, ALIMONY, SUPPORT, COUNSEL FEES OR DIVISION OF PROPERTY YOU SHOULD NOTIFY THE CLERK IN WRITING.

IF AN ORDER FOR PAYMENT OF MONEY IS ENTERED AGAINST YOU, YOUR EMPLOYER MAY BE ORDERED TO PAY PART OF YOUR WAGES TO THE PLAINTIFF OR YOUR PERSONAL PROPERTY, INCLUDING BANK ACCOUNTS, AND YOUR REAL ESTATE MAY BE TAKEN TO SATISFY THE JUDGMENT.

IF YOU INTEND TO OPPOSE THE DIVORCE, **DO NOT FAIL TO ANSWER WITHIN THE REQUIRED TIME.**

If you believe you have a defense to the Plaintiff's Complaint or if you believe you have a claim of your own against the Plaintiff, you may wish to talk to a lawyer. If you feel you cannot afford to pay a fee to a lawyer, you may ask a Clerk of the District Court for information as to places where you may seek legal assistance.

This Summons is issued by: Mary Godbout
Clerk of the District Court

Dated: ____________

Division of ____________

____
(Attorney for) Plaintiff

Served on ____________
(Date)

____
Address

____
Deputy Sheriff

____
Telephone

DCCV-2 Rev. (5/85)

STATE OF MAINE

_______________ County

On the _______________ day of _______________, 19____, I made service of the Complaint and within Summons upon the Defendant_______________ by delivering a copy of this Summons and of the Complaint to the Defendant in hand at _______________

____

(place of delivery)

Service:

Travel, _______________ miles one way $_______________
Postage $_______________
Amount $_______________

____
Deputy Sheriff

FEDERAL AFFIDAVIT

STATE OF MAINE

_______________ County
(Indicate County Where Issued)

District Court
Division of _______________
Location _______________
Docket Number _______________

Plaintiff

vs.

FEDERAL AFFIDAVIT

Defendant

I, _______________ Plaintiff, or _______________ attorney of record for the Plaintiff in the above-entitled action, on Oath depose and say on my own knowledge, that the Defendant _______________

____

____

____
(Facts, i.e.: Residence, Employment, etc.)

And at this date the said Defendant _______________ is not in the Military Service of the United States, as defined in Article I of the "Soldiers' and Sailors' Relief Act of 1940," as amended.

____

____

____
(Facts as to residence of Plaintiff or Defendant or place of service of process, etc.)

AND FURTHER REPRESENTS the Affiant under Oath that the facts showing that venue was properly laid at the place where this action was brought are as follows:

____

____

____
(Attorney for) Plaintiff

STATE OF MAINE

_______________ County _______________, 19_____

Personally appeared the above-named _______________ and made Oath that the foregoing Affidavit by him/her is true.

Before me, _______________
Notary Public/Attorney at Law

DCCV-22 Rev. (1/83)

STATE OF MAINE

SUPERIOR COURT
______________________, ss.
Docket No.______________________

DISTRICT COURT
Division of ______________________
Location ______________________
Docket No. ______________________

Plaintiff

vs.

Defendant

AFFIDAVIT AND APPLICATION TO PROCEED IN FORMA PAUPERIS

I, ______________________________________, request leave of court to proceed in forma pauperis.

1. I am without the funds to pay the filing fee and service costs.

   My monthly income is $______________.

   My necessary monthly expenses are $______________.

2. I possess no other source from which the filing or service fees can be paid.

3. I bring this action or defense in good faith.

4. I agree to reimburse any fee or service costs which have been waived or paid if at any time during the pendency of the action I am financially able to do so.

Dated:______________________ ______________________________

Personally appeared the above named affiant, and made oath, to the truth of the foregoing affidavit, signed before me.

Dated:______________________ ______________________________
Notary Public/Attorney

ORDER

The court finds that the above named affiant is proceeding in good faith and is without sufficient funds to pay the filing fee, service costs or removal fee.

It is ORDERED that the filing (removal) fee is waived.

It is ORDERED that the service costs be paid as an administrative expense.

Dated:______________________ ______________________________
Judge, District Court
Justice, Superior Court

SC-2/DCCV-4 (1/86)
CV-34 (1/86)

STATE OF MAINE

SUPERIOR COURT
______________________, ss.
Docket No.______________

DISTRICT COURT
Division of ______________
Location ______________
Docket No. ______________

Plaintiff

vs.

Defendant

AFFIDAVIT
CONCERNING CHILD CUSTODY
(TITLE 19, M.R.S.A. SEC. 810)

1. This proceeding involves a request for the court to determine the custody of ______________
______________ Date of Birth ______________
______________ Date of Birth ______________
______________ Date of Birth ______________
______________ Date of Birth ______________

2. The present address of said child(ren) is ______________
____

3. The following is a complete list of the places where said child(ren) have lived within the past five years, and the names and *present address* of all persons with whom said child(ren) have lived during that period:

Dates of Residence	Place (City and State)	Person with whom child(ren) have lived: Name	Person with whom child(ren) have lived: Present Address

4. The undersigned has not participated as a party, witness or in any other capacity in other litigation concerning the custody of said child(ren), in this or any other State, except as follows: ______________
____
____
____
____

THE UNDERSIGNED WILL ADVISE THE COURT OF ANY SUCH HEARING ARISING HEREAFTER.

DCCV-35 Rev. (1/86)
CV-40 (1/86)

5. There is no person, not a party to the present proceeding, who has physical custody of said child(ren), or claims to have custody or visiting rights with respect to said child(ren), except as follows: ______________________

____

____

____

____

The undersigned under oath and subject to the penalties of perjury, hereby declares that the statements made herein are true, upon the personal knowledge, information and belief of the undersigned, and so far as upon information and belief, that the undersigned believes them to be true.

Signed ______________________________________

Address ______________________________________

____

STATE OF MAINE

______________________________ County

Personally appeared the above named ____
and signed and made oath to the foregoing affidavit, before me,

Dated ______________________________

____
Notary Public/Attorney at Law

STATE OF MAINE

Superior Court
______________________, ss.
Docket No. ______________

District Court
Division of ______________
Location ______________
Docket No. ______________

Plaintiff

vs.

CONDITIONAL ORDER OF INCOME WITHHOLDING (19 M.R.S.A. §777)

Defendant

This Conditional Order of Income Withholding is incorporated in, and is a part of, the [Divorce Judgment] [Order] of this court dated ______________ .

It is ORDERED that the payor of income to ______________________________
(obligor)
from any source shall withhold from any amounts due the obligor, and shall pay to the Maine Department of Human Services, at least monthly, the sum of $__________ per __________, which is the obligor's current support and/or alimony obligation, together with an additional sum to be applied toward any arrearage of support or alimony owed by the obligor, notice of which has been served on the payor with a copy of this withholding order. However, the total amount withheld by the payor shall not be greater than the maximum allowed by 19 M.R.S.A. §502 and 15 U.S.C. § 1673. So long as any arrearage remains outstanding, the amount of withholding by the payor shall be the maximum permitted by these statutes.

It is further ORDERED that ______________________________ shall not serve
(obligee)
a copy of this withholding order on any payor of income until the provisions of 19 M.R.S.A. §777(1)(B)(1),(2),(4) and (5) have been met.

IMPORTANT NOTICE TO______________________________:
Withholding of your income may result if you fail to make the support or alimony payments that the court has ordered you to make. However, no withholding shall take place until the following conditions are met:

(1) You request the withholding of your income, or

(2) Your child support or alimony payments are in arrears in an amount equal to one month's support or alimony and you are notified of that arrearage in writing.

(3) The obligee must give you written notice of the amount of the arrearages at least 20 days before serving a copy of this order on the payor of income. During the 20 day period you may dispute the amount of the arrearage by filing a motion in this court asking the court to determine the amount in arrears. At the same time you may ask the court for a stay (delay) of service of this order on the payor. The court may issue a stay of not more than 60 days.

It is further ORDERED that this order be noted upon the docket by incorporation by reference pursuant to Rule 79(a).

Dated: ______________________

____
Judge, District Court
Justice, Superior Court

DCCV-45 1-87
CV-51 1-87

RULE 80(n) PROPERTY LIST

[Mark with an X all items in dispute]

REAL PROPERTY (land, land and buildings):

Located at:____

Described in deed of _______________ to _______________,

dated ____________ and recorded in _____________ County

Registry of Deeds, Book _______, Page _____________.

This real property is (marital)(non-marital of ______).

(If more than one deed, attach a list with similar information.

PERSONAL PROPERTY (clothing, furniture, vehicles, recreational equipment, bank accounts, stock, and other personal property. General references often will be sufficient and each individual item usually need not be listed.)

Items of Property	Check if marital	If non-marital, list owner

DATE______________________________

____
Signature

PETITION AND ORDER FOR MILITARY CERTIFICATION

STATE OF MAINE

_______________ County
(Indicate County Where Issued)

Plaintiff

vs.

Defendant

District Court
Division of _______________
Location _______________
Docket Number _______________

PETITION AND ORDER FOR
MILITARY CERTIFICATION

RESPECTFULLY REPRESENTS _______________
of _______________ in the County of _______________ and State of _______________
that he married _______________ of _______________
at _______________ in the County of _______________ and State of _______________
on _______________, 19_______.

That it is impossible to ascertain by reasonable diligence the whereabouts of the said _______________
_______________ whose date of birth _______________,
Social Security number _______________, service number _______________ and other identifying characteristics are as follows: _______________
____
____

WHEREFORE IT IS RESPECTFULLY REQUESTED that this Honorable Court will issue an Order to the Adjutant General of the United States Army; Chief of Staff, United States Air force, Washington, D.C.; the Chief, Bureau of Naval Personnel, Department of the Navy, Washington, D.C.; Commandant, United States Marine Corps, Washington, D.C.; and to the Commandant, United States Coast Guard, Headquarters, Washington, D.C., directing them to issue certificates as provided for by Section 601 of the Soldiers and Sailors Civil Relief Act of 1940.

____
Plaintiff

Address reply to: _______________
____
____

ORDER

Upon the foregoing Petition and after a hearing, it is hereby ORDERED, ADJUDGED AND DECREED that attested copies of said Petition and of the Order issue to the Adjutant General of the United States Army; Chief of Staff, United States Air Force, Washington, D.C.; the Chief, Bureau of Naval Personnel, Department of the Navy, Washington, D.C.; Commandant, United States Marine Corps, Washington, D.C.; and to the Commandant, United States Coast Guard, Headquarters, Washington, D.C., directing them to issue certificates provided for by Section 601 of the Soldiers and Sailors Civil Relief Act of 1940.

____
Judge of District Court

DCCV-23 Rev. (1/83)

STATE OF MAINE

District Court
Division of ______________________
Location ______________________
Docket No. ______________________

Plaintiff

vs.

DIVORCE JUDGMENT

Defendant

Notice of the pendency of this action for divorce has been duly and seasonably given according to law. This action was heard before me and the allegations and the evidence were fully presented and considered. A divorce from the bonds of matrimony is hereby ORDERED and ADJUDGED to ______________________ from ______________________ for the cause of ______________________

____

____

The counterclaim/complaint is dismissed.

The clerk is directed to incorporate this judgment by reference in the docket for this case.

Dated:

____
District Court Judge

A true copy,

Attest:

____
(Deputy) Clerk

DCCV-17 Rev. (1/86)

STATE OF MAINE

DISTRICT COURT
Division ______________________
Location ______________________
Docket No. ______________________

Plaintiff

v.

DIVORCE JUDGMENT

Defendant

1. Notice of this action for divorce has been given according to law. This action was heard before me, and the allegations and the evidence were fully presented and considered. A divorce from the bonds of matrimony is hereby ORDERED to the (parties) ______________________ for the cause of (irreconcilable marital differences) ______________________.

☐ 2. It is further ORDERED that the terms of a settlement agreement between the parties, dated ______________________, are approved and incorporated herein.

☐ 3. With respect to their minor child(ren), namely ______________________

____

it is ORDERED that (allocated) (shared) (sole) parental rights and responsibilities are awarded to ______________________ as follows:

☐ 4. The right is given to ______________________ to have contact with and by said child(ren) at all reasonable and proper times.

☐ 5. It is further ORDERED that ______________________ shall have reasonable rights of access to said child(ren).

☐ 6. It is further ORDERED that ______________________ pay to ______________________ the sum of $______________ for each child per week toward the support of said child(ren), the first payment to be made ______________, 19 ______, and payment shall be made to the State of Maine Department of Human Services for all periods that ______________________ receives Aid to Dependent Children for such child(ren).

☐ 7. It is further ORDERED that ______________________ maintain medical insurance for such child(ren) and pay ______________ all reasonable medical, hospital, optical and dental expenses for such child(ren).

☐ 8. It is further ORDERED that each parent shall have access to records and information pertaining to the child(ren), including, but not limited to, medical, dental and school records.

☐ 9. It is further ORDERED that ______________________ pay to ______________________ as alimony the sum of $______________________.

DCCV-16 Rev. (1/86)

☐ 10. It is further ORDERED that the following property be set aside or awarded as follows:

☐ 11. It is further ORDERED

☐ 12. (Plaintiff) (Defendant) is granted the right to change her name to ____________________

☐ 13. It is further ORDERED that ____________________ pay to ____________________ the sum of $__________ as counsel fees, execution to issue.

☐ 14. The clerk is directed to incorporate this judgment by reference in the docket book.

Date: ____________________

____
Judge, District Court

A true copy,
Attest:

____
(Deputy) Clerk

STATE OF MAINE

SUPERIOR COURT
____________________, ss.
Docket No. ________________

DISTRICT COURT
Division of ________________
Location ________________
Docket No. ________________

ABSTRACT OF DIVORCE DECREE

I, ____________________, the duly appointed, qualified and acting Clerk of the ____________________ Court, __________ County/Division, hereby certify that on the ________ day of ________________, 19____, a decree of divorce became final between ______________________________, Plaintiff, of____________, ______________; and____________________, Defendant, of____________, ____________, and that the following is a true copy of so much of said decree as relates to the disposition or transfer of real estate in ________________ County, Viz:

IN WITNESS WHEREOF, I have hereunto set my hand and affixed the seal of said ____________ Court this__________ day of ____________________, 19____.

(SEAL)

____
Title: Clerk, Court

NAME: ________________________

This certificate to be recorded in the Registry of Deeds for the county above named.

Return to:

____

____

____

DCCV-20 Rev. (1/86)
CV-39 (1/86)

ORDER PENDING DIVORCE

STATE OF MAINE

_______________ County
(Indicate County Where Issued)

District Court
Division of _______________
Location _______________
Docket Number _______________

Plaintiff

vs.

ORDER PENDING DIVORCE

Defendant

HEARING HAD: on the _______________ day of _______________, 19 _______

It is ORDERED and DECREED that the temporary care and custody of the minor child(ren) _______________

____

be given to the aforesaid _______________ until further order of Court, with the right given to the said _______________ to visit with said child(ren) and to be visited by said child(ren) at all reasonable times and places.

It is further ORDERED that the aforesaid _______________ pay to the aforesaid _______________ for support of each minor child _______________

____

the sum of $ _______________ per week, first payment to be made _______________ and each and every week thereafter until further order of Court, payment to be made to the Maine Department of Human Services during such time as Plaintiff/Defendant is receiving state assistance.

It is further ORDERED:

It is further ORDERED that the aforesaid _______________ pay to _______________ for counsel fees incurred in the prosecution of this Petition the sum of _______________ dollars.

Dated: _______________ _______________
Judge of District Court

DCCV-15 Rev. (1/83)

AMENDMENT TO DIVORCE JUDGMENT

STATE OF MAINE

________________________ County
(Indicate County Where Issued)

District Court
Division of ____________
Location ____________
Docket Number ____________

Plaintiff

vs.

AMENDMENT TO DIVORCE JUDGMENT

Defendant

HEARING HAD UPON THE MOTION OF THE____________:

It is hereby ORDERED and ADJUDGED that the original Divorce Judgment dated ____________ ____________ be and hereby is altered and ammended by striking out the words:

and inserting in place thereof the words:

in all other respects the original Judgment to remain in full force and effect.

Dated: ____________

____
Judge of District Court

DCCV-18 Rev. (1/83)

STATE OF MAINE

SUPERIOR COURT
______________________, ss.
CV-______________________

DISTRICT COURT
Division of ______________________
Location ______________________
Docket No. ______________________

Plaintiff

vs.

AFFIDAVIT of INCOME and ASSETS

Defendant

Name ______________________ Social Security No. ______________________
Address ______________________
Street *Town* *State* *Zip*

GROSS INCOME

1. WAGES, SALARY, SELF-EMPLOYMENT INCOME

(Attach a copy of your most recent W-2 Form and your most recent pay stub.)

How much did you earn in the last calendar year? $__________

How much have you earned so far this year?

Employer	Dates	Amount

Estimated total of wages, salary, self-employment income this year $__________

2. OTHER INCOME

List any other income received last year from any source such as alimony, social security, unemployment benefits, workers' compensation, disability, pension income, insurance, rental or mortgage income, bonuses, interest, dividends, capital gains or money from any other source except AFDC, SSI, general assistance or food stamps:

Source	Dates	Amount

Total $__________

3. FRINGE BENEFITS

List value of benefits received through employment which reduce your living expenses such as a car, housing, insurance or meals $__________

4. TOTAL ANNUAL GROSS INCOME $__________

(Add the amounts from 1, 2 and 3 above)

DCCV-51 (7/90)

PROPERTY AND ASSETS

5. VEHICLES

List any motor vehicles, including motorcycles, snowmobiles, boats, etc. Attach a separate sheet if needed.

Item	Value	Amount owed on item	Net value

6. PERSONAL PROPERTY

List any item of personal property worth more that $3000 such as gems, works of art, furniture, antiques, collections, or other items of investment vaule. Attach a separate sheet if needed.

Item	Value	Amount owed on item	Net value

7. REAL ESTATE

List all real estate that you own, including your home. Attach a separate sheet if needed.

Description and location	Value	Mortgage	Net value

8. BANK ACCOUNTS

List all accounts you have in financial institutions, such as banks, credit unions. Include savings and checking accounts, certificates of deposit, etc. Attach a separate sheet if needed.

Name of financial institution	Type of account	Amount

9. OTHER PROPERTY

List separately other property such as stocks, bonds, notes, trusts, annuities, pensions, deferred compensation, IRAs, or money that people owe you. Attach a separate sheet if needed.

Property	Value

EXPENSES RELATING TO CHILD SUPPORT WORKSHEET

11. CHILD SUPPORT

List child support you pay for children who are not a subject of this action

Name of child	To whom paid	Weekly amount
____________	____________	________
____________	____________	________
____________	____________	________

12. OTHER CHILDREN

List other children living in your home who are not the subject of this action and whom you are legally obligated to support.

Name of child	Date of birth	Relationship to you	Name of child	Date of birth	Relationship to you
________	________	________	________	________	________
________	________	________	________	________	________

13. MEDICAL INSURANCE

Cost of medical insurance you pay for yourself per year ________

Additional cost of medical insurance you pay for your children per year ________

Total ________

14. CHILD CARE COSTS

Amount of weekly child care costs you pay so you can work (or train to work) ________

15. EXTRAORDINARY MEDICAL EXPENSES

Name of child	Reason for expense	Weekly amount
____________	____________	________
____________	____________	________

16. OTHER EXPENSES

List any other large debts you owe or other exceptionally high expenses for you or your children that you feel justify a deviation from the Child Support Guidelines.

____

____

____

☒ I have attached a copy of my most recent W-2 form. ☐ I have attached a copy of my most recent pay stub.

The above financial statement is complete and includes all assets and income I receive and is based on my own personal knowledge, information and belief, and to the extent it is based on information and belief, I believe such information to be true.

Dated: ____________________

____
Signature

Personally appeared the above named ______________________________ and made oath to the foregoing affidavit, before me:

Dated: ____________________

____
(Attorney) (Notary Public) (Deputy Clerk)

A COPY OF THIS AFFIDAVIT AND THE CHILD SUPPORT WORKSHEET MUST BE PROVIDED TO THE OTHER PARTY BEFORE MEDIATION. THIS AFFIDAVIT AND THE CHILD SUPPORT WORKSHEET MUST BE FILED WITH THE COURT CLERK 3 DAYS BEFORE THE COURT HEARING.

STATE OF MAINE

SUPERIOR COURT
______________________, ss.
CV-______________________

DISTRICT COURT
Division of ______________________
Docket No. ______________________

Plaintiff

vs.

CHILD SUPPORT WORKSHEET

Defendant

Children	Date of Birth	Children		Date of Birth
		Primary Care Provider Name:	Non-Primary Care Provider Name:	Combined
1. Annual Gross Income		$	$	
a. Minus preexisting support 19 M.R.S.A. §311(5)(E)				
b. Minus health insurance premium §311(5)(F)				
c. Minus responsibility for other children of non-primary care provider §316(4)(A)				
2. Annual Gross Income (Adjusted)		$	$	$
3. Proportional Share of Gross Income (each parent's income divided by combined income)		%	%	

4. Basic Weekly Support Entitlement from Table:

Children 0 --11 Category:
(a) Total No. Children ______ at Combined Gross Income (Adjusted) per table (b) $________
(c) Number of children 0--11 ________ x amount at (b) $____________ = (d) $________

Children 12 --17 Category:
(a) Total No. Children ______ at Combined Gross Income (Adjusted) per table (e) $________
(f) Number of children 12--17 ________ x amount at (e) $____________ = (g) $________

Basic Weekly Support Entitlement: *(Sum of (d) and (g))* = (h) $________

5. Weekly Child Care and Extraordinary Medical Expenses

Child Care Costs: (19 M.R.S.A. § 316(2)(A)
Name and amount per child per week: ______________________ $____________
______________________ $____________
______________________ $____________
___ ______________________ $____________ = (i) $________

Recurring Extraordinary Medical Expenses: (19 M.R.S.A. § 316(2)(B)
Name and amount per child per week: ______________________ $____________ = (j) $________

TOTAL WEEKLY SUPPORT OBLIGATION: *(Sum of (h), (i) and (j)* = (k) $________

6. Weekly Parental Support Obligation *Line 3 times (k)*	Primary care provider spends directly	Non-primary care provider pays as support
	$	$

Submitted By: ______________________________
~~(Attorney for)~~ (Plantiff) ~~(Defendant)~~

DCCV-50 (7/90)

APPENDIX IV: COURT & COUNTY LOCATOR

This locator has been prepared to help you find the proper court in which to begin your divorce action. Simply look up the city or town, from which you wish to proceed, in this index and it will refer you to the proper court. You will also find the District Number of the Court, its Division, location and county - all information that you will need when filling out your papers.

This list is accurate to the best of our knowledge; however, when compiling such a list, there is always the possibility of misplacing a town or two. To be certain that you are in the correct place, we recommend that you check with the court clerk.

TOWN	DIST.	DIVISION	LOCATION	COUNTY
Abbott	13	Piscataquis	Dover-Foxcroft	Piscataquis
Acton	10	Western York	Sanford	York
Addison	4	Southern Washington	Machias	Washington
Albion	7	Northern Kennebec	Waterville	Kennebec
Alfred	10	Western York	Sanford	York
Alna	6	Lincoln	Wiscasset	Lincoln
Andover	11	Northern Oxford	Rumford	Oxford
Anson	12	Somerset	Skowhegan	Somerset
Appleton	6	Knox	Rockland	Knox
Ashland	2	Central Aroostook	Presque Isle	Aroostook
Athens	12	Somerset	Skowhegan	Somerset
Auburn	8	Southern Androscoggin	Auburn	Androscoggin
Augusta	7	Southern Kennebec	Augusta	Kennebec
Aurora	5	Central Hancock	Ellsworth	Hancock
Bancroft	2	Southern Aroostook	Houlton	Aroostook
Bangor	3	Southern Penobscot	Bangor	Penobscot
Bar Harbor	5	Southern Hancock	Bar Harbor	Hancock
Baring	4	Northern Washington	Calais	Washington
Bass Harbor	5	Southern Hancock	Bar Harbor	Hancock
Bath	6	Sagadahoc	Bath	Sagadahoc
Beals	4	Southern Washington	Machias	Washington
Belfast	5	Waldo	Belfast	Waldo
Belgrade	7	Northern Kennebec	Waterville	Kennebec
Belgrade Lakes	7	Northern Kennebec	Waterville	Kennebec
Benedicta	2	Southern Aroostook	Houlton	Aroostook
Benton	7	Northern Kennebec	Waterville	Kennebec
Berwick	10	Western York	Sanford	York
Bethel	11	Northern Oxford	Rumford	Oxford
Biddeford	10	Eastern York	Biddeford	York
Biddeford Pool	10	Eastern York	Biddeford	York
Bingham	12	Somerset	Skowhegan	Somerset
Blaine	2	Central Aroostook	Presque Isle	Aroostook
Blue Hill	5	Central Hancock	Ellsworth	Hancock
Boothbay	6	Lincoln	Wiscasset	Lincoln
Boothbay Harbor	6	Lincoln	Wiscasset	Lincoln
Bowdoinham	6	Sagadahoc	Bath	Sagadahoc
Bowerbank	13	Piscataquis	Dover-Foxcroft	Piscataquis
Bradford	12	Western Penobscot	Newport	Penobscot
Bradley	3	Southern Penobscot	Bangor	Penobscot
Brewer	3	Southern Penobscot	Bangor	Penobscot
Bridgewater	2	Southern Aroostook	Houlton	Aroostook
Bridgton	9	Northern Cumberland	Bridgton	Cumberland
Bristol	6	Lincoln	Wiscasset	Lincoln
Brooklin	5	Central Hancock	Ellsworth	Hancock
Brooks	5	Waldo	Belfast	Waldo
Brooksville	5	Central Hancock	Ellsworth	Hancock
Brookton	4	Northern Washington	Calais	Washington
Brownfield	9	Northern Cumberland	Bridgton	Cumberland
Brownville	13	Piscataquis	Dover-Foxcroft	Piscataquis
Brownville Junction	13	Piscataquis	Dover-Foxcroft	Piscataquis
Brunswick	8	Eastern Cumberland	Brunswick	Cumberland
Buckfield	11	Southern Oxford	South Paris	Oxford
Bucksport	5	Central Hancock	Ellsworth	Hancock
Burlington	13	Central Penobscot	Lincoln	Penobscot
Burnham	5	Waldo	Belfast	Waldo

Calais	4	Northern Washington	Calais	Washington
Cambridge	12	Somerset	Skowhegan	Somerset
Camden	6	Knox	Rockland	Knox
Canaan	12	Somerset	Skowhegan	Somerset
Canton	11	Northern Oxford	Rumford	Oxford
Cape Cottage	9	Southern Cumberland	Portland	Cumberland
Cape Elizabeth	9	Southern Cumberland	Portland	Cumberland
Cape Neddick	10	Southern York	Kittery	York
Caratunk	12	Somerset	Skowhegan	Somerset
Caribou	1	Eastern Aroostook	Caribou	Aroostook
Carmel	12	Western Penobscot	Newport	Penobscot
Casco	9	Northern Cumberland	Bridgton	Cumberland
Castine	5	Central Hancock	Ellsworth	Hancock
Center Lovell	11	Southern Oxford	South Paris	Oxford
Charleston	12	Western Penobscot	Newport	Penobscot
Cherryfield	4	Southern Washington	Machias	Washington
China	7	Southern Kennebec	Augusta	Kennebec
Chisholm	11	Franklin	Farmington	Franklin
Clinton	7	Northern Kennebec	Waterville	Kennebec
Columbia Falls	4	Southern Washington	Machias	Washington
Corinna	12	Western Penobscot	Newport	Penobscot
Cornish	10	Western York	Sanford	York
Cranberry Isles	5	Southern Hancock	Bar Harbor	Hancock
Cumberland	9	Southern Cumberland	Portland	Cumberland
Cutler	4	Southern Washington	Machias	Washington
Damariscotta	6	Lincoln	Wiscasset	Lincoln
Danforth	4	Northern Washington	Calais	Washington
Deer Isle	5	Central Hancock	Ellsworth	Hancock
Denmark	9	Northern Cumberland	Bridgton	Cumberland
Dennysville	4	Southern Washington	Machias	Washington
Detroit	12	Somerset	Skowhegan	Somerset
Dexter	12	Western Penobscot	Newport	Penobscot
Dixfield	11	Northern Oxford	Rumford	Oxford
Dixmont	12	Western Penobscot	Newport	Penobscot
Dover-Foxcroft	13	Piscataquis	Dover-Foxcroft	Piscataquis
Dresden	6	Lincoln	Wiscasset	Lincoln
Eagle Lake	1	Western Aroostook	Madawaska	Aroostook
East Andover	11	Northern Oxford	Rumford	Oxford
East Baldwin	9	Northern Cumberland	Bridgton	Cumberland
East Boothbay	6	Lincoln	Wiscasset	Lincoln
East Dixfield	11	Franklin	Farmington	Franklin
East Lebanon	10	Western York	Sanford	York
East Machias	4	Southern Washington	Machias	Washington
East Millinocket	13	Northern Penobscot	Millinocket	Penobscot
East Parsonfield	10	Western York	Sanford	York
East Peru	11	Northern Oxford	Rumford	Oxford
East Sebago	9	Northern Cumberland	Bridgton	Cumberland
East Stoneham	11	Southern Oxford	South Paris	Oxford
East Sumner	11	Southern Oxford	South Paris	Oxford
East Vassalboro	7	Northern Kennebec	Waterville	Kennebec
East Waterboro	10	Western York	Sanford	York
East Wilton	11	Franklin	Farmington	Franklin
Easton	2	Central Aroostook	Presque Isle	Aroostook
Eastport	4	Northern Washington	Calais	Washington
Edgecomb	6	Lincoln	Wiscasset	Lincoln
Eliot	10	Southern York	Kittery	York
Ellsworth	5	Central Hancock	Ellsworth	Hancock

Enfield	13	Central Penobscot	Lincoln	Penobscot
Etna	12	Western Penobscot	Newport	Penobscot
Eustis	11	Franklin	Farmington	Franklin
Exeter	12	Western Penobscot	Newport	Penobscot
Fairfield	12	Somerset	Skowhegan	Somerset
Falmouth	9	Southern Cumberland	Portland	Cumberland
Farmington	11	Franklin	Farmington	Franklin
Farmington Falls	11	Franklin	Farmington	Franklin
Fayette	7	Northern Kennebec	Waterville	Kennebec
Forest City	4	Northern Washington	Calais	Washington
Fort Fairfield	2	Central Aroostook	Presque Isle	Aroostook
Fort Kent	1	Western Aroostook	Madawaska	Aroostook
Franklin	5	Central Hancock	Ellsworth	Hancock
Frankfort	5	Waldo	Belfast	Waldo
Freedom	5	Waldo	Belfast	Waldo
Freeport	8	Eastern Cumberland	Brunswick	Cumberland
Frenchville	1	Western Aroostook	Madawaska	Aroostook
Friendship	6	Knox	Rockland	Knox
Fryeburg	9	Northern Cumberland	Bridgton	Cumberland
Gardiner	7	Southern Kennebec	Augusta	Kennebec
Garland	12	Western Penobscot	Newport	Penobscot
Georgetown	6	Sagadahoc	Bath	Sagadahoc
Gorham	9	Southern Cumberland	Portland	Cumberland
Gouldsboro	5	Central Hancock	Ellsworth	Hancock
Grand Isle	1	Western Aroostook	Madawaska	Aroostook
Grand Lake Stream	4	Northern Washington	Calais	Washington
Gray	9	Southern Cumberland	Portland	Cumberland
Greene	8	Southern Androscoggin	Lewiston	Androscoggin
Green Lake	5	Central Hancock	Ellsworth	Hancock
Greenville Junction	13	Piscataquis	Dover-Foxcroft	Piscataquis
Guilford	13	Piscataquis	Dover-Foxcroft	Piscataquis
Hallowell	7	Southern Kennebec	Augusta	Kennebec
Hampden	3	Southern Penobscot	Bangor	Penobscot
Hancock	5	Central Hancock	Ellsworth	Hancock
Hanover	11	Northern Oxford	Rumford	Oxford
Harmony	12	Somerset	Skowhegan	Somerset
Harpswell	8	Eastern Cumberland	Brunswick	Cumberland
Harrington	4	Southern Washington	Machias	Washington
Harrison	9	Northern Cumberland	Bridgton	Cumberland
Hartland	12	Somerset	Skowhegan	Somerset
Haynesville	2	Southern Aroostook	Houlton	Aroostook
Hebron	11	Southern Oxford	South Paris	Oxford
Hiram	9	Northern Cumberland	Bridgton	Cumberland
Hodgdon	2	Southern Aroostook	Houlton	Aroostook
Hollis Center	10	Eastern York	Biddeford	York
Hope	6	Knox	Rockland	Knox
Houlton	2	Southern Aroostook	Houlton	Aroostook
Howland	13	Central Penobscot	Lincoln	Penobscot
Hudson	12	Western Penobscot	Newport	Penobscot
Indian Township	4	Northern Washington	Calais	Washington
Island Falls	2	Southern Aroostook	Houlton	Aroostook
Isle au Haut	6	Knox	Rockland	Knox
Isleboro	5	Waldo	Belfast	Waldo
Jackman	12	Somerset	Skowhegan	Somerset
Jay	11	Franklin	Farmington	Franklin

Jefferson	6	Lincoln	Wiscasset	Lincoln
Jonesboro	4	Southern Washington	Machias	Washington
Jonesport	4	Southern Washington	Machias	Washington
Kenduskeag	12	Western Penobscot	Newport	Penobscot
Kennebunk	10	Eastern York	Biddeford	York
Kennebunk Beach	10	Eastern York	Biddeford	York
Kennebunkport	10	Eastern York	Biddeford	York
Kezar Falls	10	Western York	Sanford	York
Kingfield	11	Franklin	Farmington	Franklin
Kingman	13	Central Penobscot	Lincoln	Penobscot
Kittery	10	Southern York	Kittery	York
Kittery Point	10	Southern York	Kittery	York
LaGrange	13	Central Penobscot	Lincoln	Penobscot
Lambert Lake	4	Northern Washington	Calais	Washington
Lee	13	Central Penobscot	Lincoln	Penobscot
Levant	12	Western Penobscot	Newport	Penobscot
Lewiston	8	Southern Androscoggin	Lewiston	Androscoggin
Liberty	5	Waldo	Belfast	Waldo
Limerick	10	Western York	Sanford	York
Limestone	1	Eastern Aroostook	Caribou	Aroostook
Limington	10	Western York	Sanford	York
Lincoln	13	Central Penobscot	Lincoln	Penobscot
Lincolnville	5	Waldo	Belfast	Waldo
Lincolnville Center	5	Waldo	Belfast	Waldo
Linneus	2	Southern Aroostook	Houlton	Aroostook
Lisbon	8	Southern Androscoggin	Lewiston	Androscoggin
Lisbon Center	8	Southern Androscoggin	Lewiston	Androscoggin
Lisbon Falls	8	Southern Androscoggin	Lewiston	Androscoggin
Litchfield	7	Southern Kennebec	Augusta	Kennebec
Livermore	11	Northern Androscoggin	Livermore Falls	Androscoggin
Livermore Falls	11	Northern Androscoggin	Livermore Falls	Androscoggin
Lovell	9	Northern Cumberland	Bridgton	Oxford
Lubec	4	Southern Washington	Machias	Washington
Machias	4	Southern Washington	Machias	Washington
Machiasport	4	Southern Washington	Machias	Washington
Madawaska	1	Western Aroostook	Madawaska	Aroostook
Madison	12	Somerset	Skowhegan	Somerset
Manchester	7	Southern Kennebec	Augusta	Kennebec
Mapleton	2	Central Aroostook	Presque Isle	Aroostook
Mars Hill	2	Central Aroostook	Presque Isle	Aroostook
Masardis	2	Central Aroostook	Presque Isle	Aroostook
Matinicus	6	Knox	Rockland	Knox
Mattawamkeag	13	Central Penobscot	Lincoln	Penobscot
Mechanic Falls	8	Southern Androscoggin	Lewiston	Androscoggin
Meddybemps	4	Northern Washington	Calais	Washington
Medway	13	Northern Penobscot	Millinocket	Penobscot
Mercer	12	Somerset	Skowhegan	Somerset
Mexico	11	Northern Oxford	Rumford	Oxford
Millbridge	4	Southern Washington	Machias	Washington
Milford	3	Southern Penobscot	Bangor	Penobscot
Millinocket	13	Northern Penobscot	Millinocket	Penobscot
Milo	13	Piscataquis	Dover-Foxcroft	Piscataquis
Minot	8	Southern Androscoggin	Lewiston	Androscoggin
Monhegan	6	Knox	Rockland	Knox
Monmouth	7	Southern Kennebec	Augusta	Kennebec
Monroe	5	Waldo	Belfast	Waldo
Monson	13	Piscataquis	Dover-Foxcroft	Piscataquis

Morrill	5	Waldo	Belfast	Waldo
Mount Vernon	7	Northern Kennebec	Waterville	Kennebec
Naples	9	Northern Cumberland	Bridgton	Cumberland
New Gloucester	9	Southern Cumberland	Portland	Cumberland
New Limerick	2	Southern Aroostook	Houlton	Aroostook
New Portland	12	Somerset	Skowhegan	Somerset
New Sharon	11	Franklin	Farmington	Franklin
New Sweden	1	Eastern Aroostook	Caribou	Aroostook
New Vineyard	11	Franklin	Farmington	Franklin
Newcastle	6	Lincoln	Wiscasset	Lincoln
Newport	12	Western Penobscot	Newport	Penobscot
Newry	11	Northern Oxford	Rumford	Oxford
Nobleboro	6	Lincoln	Wiscasset	Lincoln
Norridgewock	12	Somerset	Skowhegan	Somerset
North Anson	12	Somerset	Skowhegan	Somerset
North Belgrade	7	Northern Kennebec	Waterville	Kennebec
North Berwick	10	Western York	Sanford	York
North Bridgton	9	Northern Cumberland	Bridgton	Cumberland
North Edgecomb	6	Lincoln	Wiscasset	Lincoln
North Fryeburg	9	Northern Cumberland	Bridgton	Oxford
North Haven	6	Knox	Rockland	Knox
North Jay	11	Franklin	Farmington	Franklin
North Leeds	11	Northern Androscoggin	Livermore Falls	Androscoggin
North Lovell	11	Southern Oxford	South Paris	Oxford
North New Portland	12	Somerset	Skowhegan	Somerset
North Shapleigh	10	Western York	Sanford	York
North Turner	11	Northern Androscoggin	Livermore Falls	Androscoggin
North Vassalboro	7	Northern Kennebec	Waterville	Kennebec
North Waterboro	10	Western York	Sanford	York
North Waterford	11	Southern Oxford	South Paris	Oxford
North Whitefield	6	Lincoln	Wiscasset	Lincoln
North Windham	9	Southern Cumberland	Portland	Cumberland
Norway	11	Southern Oxford	South Paris	Oxford
Oakfield	2	Southern Aroostook	Houlton	Aroostook
Oakland	7	Northern Kennebec	Waterville	Kennebec
Ogunquit	10	Eastern York	Biddeford	York
Old Orchard Beach	10	Eastern York	Biddeford	York
Old Town	3	Southern Penobscot	Bangor	Penobscot
Orient	2	Southern Aroostook	Houlton	Aroostook
Orland	5	Central Hancock	Ellsworth	Hancock
Orono	3	Southern Penobscot	Bangor	Penobscot
Orrington	3	Southern Penobscot	Bangor	Penobscot
Owls Head	6	Knox	Rockland	Knox
Oxford	11	Southern Oxford	South Paris	Oxford
Palermo	5	Waldo	Belfast	Waldo
Palmyra	12	Somerset	Skowhegan	Somerset
Paris	11	Southern Oxford	South Paris	Oxford
Passadumkeag	13	Central Penobscot	Lincoln	Penobscot
Patten	13	Northern Penobscot	Millinocket	Penobscot
Pembroke	4	Northern Washington	Calais	Washington
Penobscot	5	Central Hancock	Ellsworth	Hancock
Perham	1	Eastern Aroostook	Caribou	Aroostook
Perry	4	Northern Washington	Calais	Washington
Peru	11	Northern Oxford	Rumford	Oxford
Phillips	11	Franklin	Farmington	Franklin
Phippsburg	6	Sagadahoc	Bath	Sagadahoc
Pittsfield	12	Somerset	Skowhegan	Somerset

Plymouth	12	Western Penobscot	Newport	Penobscot
Poland	8	Southern Androscoggin	Lewiston	Androscoggin
Poland Spring	8	Southern Androscoggin	Lewiston	Androscoggin
Porter	9	Northern Cumberland	Bridgton	Oxford
Portland	9	Southern Cumberland	Portland	Cumberland
Pownal	8	Eastern Cumberland	Brunswick	Cumberland
Prentiss	13	Central Penobscot	Lincoln	Penobscot
Presque Isle	2	Central Aroostook	Presque Isle	Aroostook
Princeton	4	Northern Washington	Calais	Washington
Rangeley	11	Franklin	Farmington	Franklin
Raymond	9	Southern Cumberland	Portland	Cumberland
Readfield	7	Southern Kennebec	Augusta	Kennebec
Richmond	6	Sagadahoc	Bath	Sagadahoc
Robbinston	4	Northern Washington	Calais	Washington
Rockland	6	Knox	Rockland	Knox
Rockport	6	Knox	Rockland	Knox
Rockwood	12	Somerset	Skowhegan	Somerset
Roxbury	11	North Oxford	Rumford	Oxford
Rumford	11	North Oxford	Rumford	Oxford
Rumford Center	11	North Oxford	Rumford	Oxford
Rumford Point	11	North Oxford	Rumford	Oxford
Sabattus	8	Southern Androscoggin	Lewiston	Androscoggin
Saco	10	Eastern York	Biddeford	York
St. Agatha	1	Western Aroostook	Madawaska	Aroostook
St. Albans	12	Somerset	Skowhegan	Somerset
St. Francis	1	Western Aroostook	Madawaska	Aroostook
St. George	6	Knox	Rockland	Knox
Sanford	10	Western York	Sanford	York
Sangerville	13	Piscataquis	Dover-Foxcroft	Piscataquis
Scarborough	9	Southern Cumberland	Portland	Cumberland
Searsport	5	Waldo	Belfast	Waldo
Sebago Lake	9	Southern Cumberland	Portland	Cumberland
Sebec	13	Piscataquis	Dover-Foxcroft	Piscataquis
Sebec Lake	13	Piscataquis	Dover-Foxcroft	Piscataquis
Seboeis	13	Central Penobscot	Lincoln	Penobscot
Sedgwick	5	Central Hancock	Ellsworth	Hancock
Shapleigh	10	Western York	Sanford	York
Sherman	2	Southern Aroostook	Houlton	Aroostook
Shirley Mills	13	Piscataquis	Dover-Foxcroft	Piscataquis
Skowhegan	12	Somerset	Skowhegan	Somerset
Smithfield	12	Somerset	Skowhegan	Somerset
Smyrna	2	Southern Aroostook	Houlton	Aroostook
Solon	12	Somerset	Skowhegan	Somerset
Sorrento	5	Central Hancock	Ellsworth	Hancock
South Berwick	10	Southern York	Kittery	York
South Bristol	6	Lincoln	Wiscasset	Lincoln
South Casco	9	Northern Cumberland	Bridgton	Cumberland
South China	7	Southern Kennebec	Augusta	Kennebec
South Freeport	8	Eastern Cumberland	Brunswick	Cumberland
South Gardiner	7	Southern Kennebec	Augusta	Kennebec
South Harpswell	8	Eastern Cumberland	Brunswick	Cumberland
South Hiram	9	Northern Cumberland	Bridgton	Oxford
South Paris	11	Southern Oxford	South Paris	Oxford
South Portland	9	Southern Cumberland	Portland	Cumberland
South Thomaston	6	Knox	Rockland	Knox
South Waterford	11	Southern Oxford	South Paris	Oxford
Southwest Harbor	5	Southern Hancock	Bar Harbor	Hancock
South Windham	9	Southern Cumberland	Portland	Cumberland

Springfield	13	Central Penobscot	Lincoln	Penobscot
Stacyville	13	Northern Penobscot	Millinocket	Penobscot
Standish	9	Southern Cumberland	Portland	Cumberland
Stetson	12	Western Penobscot	Newport	Penobscot
Steuben	4	Southern Washington	Machias	Washington
Stockholm	1	Eastern Aroostook	Caribou	Aroostook
Stockton Springs	5	Waldo	Belfast	Waldo
Stonington	5	Central Hancock	Ellsworth	Hancock
Strong	11	Franklin	Farmington	Franklin
Sullivan	5	Central Hancock	Ellsworth	Hancock
Surry	5	Central Hancock	Ellsworth	Hancock
Swans Island	5	Southern Hancock	Bar Harbor	Hancock
Temple	11	Franklin	Farmington	Franklin
Thomaston	6	Knox	Rockland	Knox
Thorndike	5	Waldo	Belfast	Waldo
Togus	7	Southern Kennebec	Augusta	Kennebec
Topsfield	4	Northern Washington	Calais	Washington
Topsham	6	Sagadahoc	Bath	Sagadahoc
Troy	5	Waldo	Belfast	Waldo
Turner	11	Northern Androscoggin	Livermore Falls	Androscoggin
Turner Center	11	Northern Androscoggin	Livermore Falls	Androscoggin
Union	6	Knox	Rockland	Knox
Unity	5	Waldo	Belfast	Waldo
Upton	11	Northern Oxford	Rumford	Oxford
Van Buren	1	Western Aroostook	Madawaska	Aroostook
Vanceboro	4	Northern Washington	Calais	Washington
Vassalboro	7	Northern Kennebec	Waterville	Kennebec
Veazie	3	Southern Penobscot	Bangor	Penobscot
Vienna	7	Northern Kennebec	Waterville	Kennebec
Vinalhaven	6	Knox	Rockland	Knox
Waite	4	Northern Washington	Calais	Washington
Waldoboro	6	Lincoln	Wiscasset	Lincoln
Warren	6	Knox	Rockland	Knox
Washburn	1	Eastern Aroostook	Caribou	Aroostook
Washington	6	Knox	Rockland	Knox
Waterboro	10	Western York	Sanford	York
Waterford	11	Southern Oxford	South Paris	Oxford
Waterville	7	Northern Kennebec	Waterville	Kennebec
Wayne	7	Northern Kennebec	Waterville	Kennebec
Weld	11	Franklin	Farmington	Franklin
Wellington	13	Piscataquis	Dover-Foxcroft	Piscataquis
Wells	10	Eastern York	Biddeford	York
Wesley	4	Southern Washington	Machias	Washington
West Baldwin	9	Northern Cumberland	Bridgton	Cumberland
West Bethel	11	Northern Oxford	Rumford	Oxford
West Bowdoin	6	Sagadahoc	Bath	Sagadahoc
West Buxton	10	Eastern York	Biddeford	York
West Forks	12	Somerset	Skowhegan	Somerset
West Jonesport	4	Southern Washington	Machias	Washington
West Minot	8	Southern Androscoggin	Lewiston or Auburn	Androscoggin
West Newfield	10	Western York	Sanford	York
West Paris	11	Southern Oxford	South Paris	Oxford
West Peru	11	Northern Oxford	Rumford	Oxford
West Scarborough	9	Southern Cumberland	Portland	Cumberland
West Soutport	6	Lincoln	Wiscasset	Lincoln
West Sumner	11	Southern Oxford	South Paris	Oxford

Westbrook	9	Southern Cumberland	Portland	Cumberland
Westfield	2	Central Aroostook	Presque Isle	Aroostook
Weston	2	Southern Aroostook	Houlton	Aroostook
Whitefield	6	Lincoln	Wiscasset	Lincoln
Whiting	4	Southern Washington	Machias	Washington
Whitneyville	4	Southern Washington	Machias	Washington
Wilton	11	Franklin	Farmington	Franklin
Windsor	7	Southern Kennebec	Augusta	Kennebec
Winn	13	Central Penobscot	Lincoln	Penobscot
Winslow	7	Northern Kennebec	Waterville	Kennebec
Winter Harbor	5	Central Hancock	Ellsworth	Hancock
Winterport	5	Waldo	Belfast	Waldo
Winthrop	7	Southern Kennebec	Augusta	Kennebec
Wiscasset	6	Lincoln	Wiscasset	Lincoln
Woodland	1	Eastern Aroostook	Caribou	Aroostook
Woodland	4	Northern Washington	Calais	Washington
Woolwich	6	Sagadahoc	Bath	Sagadahoc
Yarmouth	8	Eastern Cumberland	Brunswick	Cumberland
York	10	Southern York	Kittery	York